Praise for *Take*

"*Take the L.E.A.P.* will encourage you to think about how you approach developing a culture of innovation in your school or classroom. Elisabeth Bostwick wraps together a wonderful blend of inspirational stories, applicable research, and her rich educational experiences. Fueled by her passion to bring more authenticity to education, she has brought us a book that will challenge traditional teaching paradigms and spark educators to shift learning that will empower students. Elisabeth also delivers practical strategies at end of each chapter, called L.E.A.P. tips, to immediately implement the next day. This book will be a gem in your collection and one you will refer back to often."

—**Todd Whitaker**, professor of educational leadership,
University of Missouri

"Elisabeth Bostwick provides compelling reasons why we need to reimagine learning and how we can cultivate an environment where risk-taking and innovation flourish. In *Take the L.E.A.P., Ignite a Culture of Innovation*, Elisabeth lays the foundation for how we can create a culture that encourages learners to connect with their interests, leading to the development of passions. As we move closer to automation and AI replacing routine jobs, this book shows how to spark curiosity, foster creativity, and empower students within their learning. However, Elisabeth doesn't just write about theory, she also shares practical tips and strategies for how you can transform traditional teaching into authentic, meaningful learning experiences. *Take the L.E.A.P.* will not only challenge your thinking, but also provide direction on how to move toward the innovation economy."

—**Don Wettrick**, founder and president of STARTedUP Foundation

"*Take the L.E.A.P.: Ignite a Culture of Innovation* seamlessly weaves best practice with practical application in the classroom. Elisabeth expertly uses relatable and poignant personal and professional stories to provide substance to concepts that can feel abstract and difficult to implement. Anyone could easily take this book and transform their classroom to increase student empowerment and creative, divergent thinking."

—**Mandy Froehlich**, director of innovation & technology, author of *The Fire Within* and *Divergent EDU*

"It is our moral imperative to encourage all learners in their journey." This poignant quote from *Take the L.E.A.P.* captures the passion of Elisabeth Bostwick to raise the bar for classrooms everywhere. Bostwick is a champion for students, and, in this important book, she inspires and empowers teachers to dig deep—to create learning experiences for students that are meaningful. She understands the stakes are high. It's not just about transforming classrooms; it's about transforming the lives of our students."

—**Danny Steele**, educator, author, and speaker, @SteeleThoughts

"If you are looking to *Ignite a Culture of Innovation*, I encourage you to *Take the L.E.A.P.* This book is an inspiring and practical roadmap for transforming teaching and learning in our classrooms and schools. Written by someone who has practiced what she preaches, *Take the L.E.A.P.* shows us how we can support both students and adults in their pursuit of more innovative and meaningful learning experiences. Now is the time to improve education. This book can help us do just that."

—**Jeffrey Zoul**, EdD, author, speaker, leadership coach, and president of ConnectEDD

"At certain times in our life we come across a book that is refreshing, bold and encouraging. *Take the L.E.A.P.: Ignite a Culture of Innovation* is one of those times! Elisabeth Bostwick takes her courage as an educator to push thinking while serving as a source of encouragement and inspiration to elevate education. Leveraging brain-based research and high-effect learning strategies, Elisabeth provides tips and strategies that will spark curiosity, cultivate divergent thinking, and empower learning! The time is now to *Take the L.E.A.P.*!

—**LaVonna Roth**, speaker, consultant, best-selling author & founder of Ignite Your S.H.I.N.E.®

"*Take the L.E.A.P.* by Elisabeth Bostwick pushes us to reshape our thinking about how we view teaching and learning and how all educators can become positive influencers in our daily work with students. This book will remind you of the important role students play in their own learning and encourage you to take a L.E.A.P. in order to create powerful, collaborative learning moments for not only your students, but yourself as well."

—**Jimmy Casas**, educator, author, speaker, and leadership coach

"Is compliance killing innovation in your classroom? If so, it's time to *Take the L.E.A.P.*! Within this gem, Elisabeth Bostwick, a practicing classroom teacher, shares practical strategies, authentic narratives, and actionable reflection inquiries that will enable your learners' innovative potential to soar. It's time to stop yielding when you reach a crossroad of compliance and begin unleashing confidence, agency, and ownership to leap forward in learning! Jump in; you won't be disappointed."

—**Tara M. Martin**, educator, keynote speaker, author of *Be REAL*

"Elisabeth's book provides meaningful reasons why educators need to embrace a new way of thinking and creation in school, for both themselves and their students. *Take the L.E.A.P.* provides actionable ideas for all levels on how to let go of ideas that no longer work in order to embrace ones that support curiosity and innovation in all levels of learning. As a current classroom teacher, this book is packed with relatable stories and suggestions that will make you think and act in powerful ways to serve students."

—**George Couros**, co-publisher for IMPress Books, educational innovation consultant, author of *The Innovator's Mindset*

"Are you ready to ignite a culture of innovation in your classroom or campus? Through the pages of her powerful book, Elisabeth Bostwick helps us to take the L.E.A.P through building a foundation of a Luminous culture, Empowered learning, Authenticity in learning, and Potential soars. This book is pure inspiration, through each page filled with heartfelt stories and practical strategies for immediate implementation."

—**Beth Houf**, proud principal at Fulton Middle School, co-author, *Lead Like a PIRATE: Make School Amazing for Your Students and Staff*

"Be prepared to take a quantum leap forward with Elisabeth Bostwick! *Take the L.E.A.P.: Ignite a Culture of Innovation* is a memorable journey into fostering a positive movement for our kids to take multiple leaps forward into creativity, innovation, and uncharted horizons. Elisabeth is your guide providing practical wisdom to empower a true culture of innovation in any classroom or schoolhouse. Her passionate voice for innovative action will resonate long after you reach the concluding pages."

—Sean Gaillard, principal and author of *The Pepper Effect: Tap into the Magic of Creativity, Culture, and Innovation*

"Too often in school, we demand compliance and expect learners to complete assignments. In *Take the L.E.A.P.*, Elisabeth Bostwick shares stories, research, and examples that will compel you to reimagine what our schools can be and inspire you to create problem-solvers and innovators who will thrive in and out of school."

—Dr. Katie Martin, VP of partnerships, AltSchool, author of *Learner-Centered Innovation*

"In *Take the L.E.A.P.*, Elisabeth Bostwick helps modern educators create the school of their students' dreams. If you find yourself struggling to create the magical classroom experience every kid deserves, or you are just looking for a fresh perspective to upgrade your teaching, this book is for you."

—Danny "Sunshine" Bauer, author of *The Better Leaders Better Schools Roadmap* and your favorite podcast host

"Elisabeth does an excellent job of taking the reader on a journey of how her WHY has impacted her as a teacher leader and as an advocate for reimagining the schooling experience for students and teachers. Through anecdotes, this book outlines reflective strategies that will challenge all educators to grow, and the tips and questions at the end of each chapter give the reader an immediate call to action. If you want to move beyond the conversation of how to make school relevant and amazing for kids, this is a must read!"

—Sanée Bell, EdD, principal in Houston, Texas

Take the L.E.A.P.

Ignite a Culture of Innovation

Elisabeth Bostwick

Take the L.E.A.P.

Published by IMPress, a division of Dave Burgess Consulting, Inc.
ImpressBooks.org
daveburgessconsulting.com

Editing and Interior Design by My Writers' Connection
Cover Design by Genesis Kohler

Library of Congress Control Number: 2018967921
Paperback ISBN: 978-1-948334-06-8
eBook ISBN: 978-1-948334-07-5
First Printing: January 2019

Dedication

For my sons, Julian and Nolan

You two inspire me to be the best I possibly can be. Believe in yourselves, be the good you wish to see in the world, and persevere through challenges to reach personal success.

Throughout your journey in life, remember these words from Ralph Waldo Emerson:

"What is success? To laugh often and much; to win the respect of intelligent people and the affection of children; to earn the appreciation of honest critics and endure the betrayal of false friends; to appreciate the beauty; to find the best in others; to leave the world a bit better, whether by a healthy child, a garden patch, or a redeemed social condition; to know even one life has breathed easier because you have lived. This is to have succeeded!"

Contents

L.E.A.P. Forward
by Tom Murray

Today's educational paradigm is more diverse than at any other point in history. The educational experience for today's Netflix Generation of students in some places remains one of compliance, control, and conformity; in other places, design thinking, creation, and deeper learning are part of the everyday experience. In some places, twenty-first-century tools are layered on top of twentieth-century pedagogy. In others, future-ready skills are developed and students are prepared for whatever it is they choose to do after high school. In some places, we school the love of learning right out of a child by the time they graduate. In others, learners leave with an *Innovator's Mindset*, ready to take on the world. So why the dichotomy?

One area of tremendous growth in educational spaces over the past few years is the advancement in the science of learning, which engages in the design and implementation of learning innovations as well as the improvement of instructional methodologies. Simply put, no longer is the regurgitation of low-level material, averaged together over time to determine an outcome, even relevant—no less does it remotely prepare students for the life ahead. Fortunately, great transformation is already underway, the type of transformation that you'll read about in the coming pages.

When filled with agency and empowered by dynamic learning experiences, today's learners can undoubtedly change the world. They are up to the challenge. Are we?

It's exactly why we must **L.E.A.P.** forward!

There's no better eye to gauge what today's learners need than through the lens of someone in classrooms every day, who has poured their heart into other people's children day in and day out. It's part of the reason that Elisabeth Bostwick is the perfect person to inspire yet challenge educators while helping them to move forward. Not only has she invested her career in the potential of young learners, but she also sees the world through the eyes of her own children. With her vast array of experiences, and her own children's future as her guiding light, Bostwick's passion for what's possible, combined with a needed sense of urgency, create a compelling manifesto to help us all to not just move forward—*but to L.E.A.P. forward.*

As Bostwick so eloquently shares, creating the learning experiences that today's modern learners need is grounded in a **Luminous Culture (L).** Simply put, in a toxic school environment, innovation will not thrive. In a culture where teachers are not able to take risks, they will retreat to areas of comfort; and, honestly, who can blame them? So who's responsible for creating such a culture of innovation in your school? You . . . alongside every adult that works there. So what do you intentionally do each day to create a culture where all students can thrive? How do you encourage those around you to step out of their comfort zones and fail forward for the students that they serve? Creating a luminous culture in your school is solidified in trust. You must strive to earn trust while building it with both your colleagues *and* your students.

These types of learning cultures give way to opportunities for innovation. It's what ultimately makes **Empowered Learning (E)** possible. With all we know about how students learn, and all that we know will be needed in their future world of work, utilizing a one-size-fits-all, sit-and-get, regurgitation-based methodology is simply educational malpractice. To unleash the next generation of innovators, we must develop agency inside our learners, so they are ready to embrace challenges and develop the creative and critical thinking skills needed to thrive in the coming decades. We must empower their learning to prepare them for their future, not our past.

Yet, if we are to truly empower learners, **Authenticity in Learning (A)** is at the core. Creating the innovative learning experiences our students need is not possible without first shining a light on each student's unique gifts and abilities. When we recognize the unique interests, talents, and passions of our students, we create a culture where students want to be engaged. More importantly, we create an inclusive culture of diverse lenses, one that embodies deeper experiences for all. When we respect the unique abilities wrapped up in each student and amplify their brilliance, today's learners can achieve far more than our adult lenses often envision. Bostwick's lens as a teacher will guide you in practical ways to develop such agency and voice for every learner in your classroom or school.

Too often these types of authentic and personal learning experiences are the exception, not the norm. Yet when learners are used to guiding all decision-making, their **Potential Soars (P)**. When done consistently over time, a dynamic legacy is built. Being an educator is the greatest profession in the world, as you get to leave your fingerprints on the lives of others for generations to come. There's no doubt that you'll be remembered, but it's *how you'll be remembered* that makes the difference. How will you unleash the potential that walks through your doors each day? What will your legacy be?

Are you ready to L.E.A.P.?

I have no doubt that, like me, you'll love this book. Throughout the words written on these pages, Bostwick will leave you inspired by her stories and empowered with practical examples as she simultaneously challenges the status quo. She'll cause you to reflect on your own practices while supporting you in creating the innovative learning experiences today's modern learners need to thrive. Are you ready?

Let's go!

All for the kids we serve,

Thomas C. Murray
director of innovation, Future Ready Schools®
best-selling co-author of ASCD's *Learning Transformed: 8 Keys to Designing Tomorrow's Schools, Today*

Are You Ready to L.E.A.P.?

Twenty years from now, you will be more
disappointed by the things you didn't do than
by the ones you did. So throw off the bowlines,
sail away from the safe harbor, catch the trade
winds in your sails. Explore. Dream. Discover.

—Mark Twain

A hand-drawn picture on our coffee table caught my eye. I recognized it as a picture drawn by our youngest child, Nolan, who was seven at the time. Noticing that one of the people drawn looked sad, I was curious about what it represented. I called out to Nolan, "Hey, buddy! What's going on here in this picture?" Nolan walked over, casually glanced at the drawing, then said nonchalantly as he walked away, "Mom, that's just me in school."

Me in school? I replayed this comment in my mind trying to make sense of it.

Determined to understand what he was feeling, I called him back. "Nolan," I asked, "why do you feel sad in school?" After looking up at me with his big blue eyes, Nolan opened up.

As we sat together, Nolan detailed his frustration with completing numerous worksheets filled with math problems he already knew how to solve and reading teacher-assigned books that did not interest him in the least. He excelled in math and had always enjoyed reading, but he was beginning to dread both. While Nolan was struggling to find purpose in school, like most children, he liked his teacher. He thought she was nice but told me, "She's happy all day because she gets to choose everything we do." It goes to show that kids know when they have autonomy versus acting out of compliance.

What really struck me that day was when Nolan pointed out that he drew a pencil with wings on it flying beside him in the classroom and proceeded to explain what it represented. Nolan said, "Momma, there are so many things I want to learn, make, and explore! But I can't; they're out of my reach but always on my mind. Those are only things I can do at home or during summer STEAM camps."

No way. Learning, making, and exploring is exactly what school is for.

Nolan's teacher was not intentionally doing anything wrong. Simply put, she was teaching the way she had been taught through her own experiences as a child or how she learned to teach. Our experiences influence the way we approach our respective roles as educators. His teacher was caring and seemed to desire to ensure all the content was covered. What happened as a result occurs in classrooms across the nation: When our attention becomes hyperfocused on content, assessments, and management, we lose touch with what matters most—the learners' voice.

My husband, Michael, and I have two sons, Julian and Nolan. From the time our boys were little, we have immersed them in exploration and fostered their natural curiosity. Watching our boys grow throughout the years and experience the world around them has been pure joy! Both have always had a deep desire to learn and were divergent or creative thinkers by nature.

Hearing Nolan describe how he felt about learning at school triggered a feeling of disheartenment. It also awoke a whole new level of understanding about how the focus in classrooms can neglect to empower student voice and choice and foster curiosity. Nolan's experience is just one chapter in his story, and I'm driven to help shape his narrative (and that of other children) by initiating conversations that spur us all to create schools that encourage and inspire our students to develop as passionate learners.

Our schools ought to be places where students explore, inquire, and create new-and-improved ideas within a supportive, collaborative environment. Of course, our learners require all the basics to be successful, but the approaches we employ are what foster empowerment.

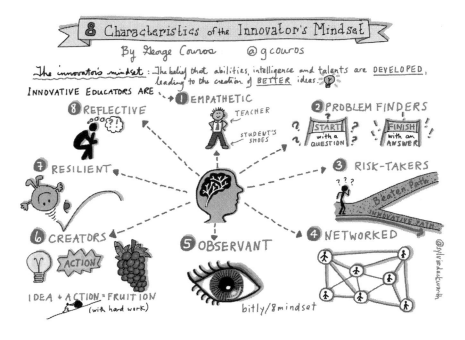

8 Characteristics of the Innovator's Mindset
By George Couros @gcouros

One approach I believe in wholeheartedly is striving to cultivate an innovator's mindset in children. In *The Innovator's Mindset*, George Couros defines this mindset as "the belief that abilities, intelligence, and talents are developed, leading to the creation of better ideas."[1] Couros explains that the *Innovator's Mindset* takes the growth mindset a step further. Whereas a growth mindset is the ability to understand that you can learn, the innovator's mindset is that you develop your learning so that you can create something with the acquired knowledge. While many schools have spent a significant amount of time exploring Carol Dweck's work on growth versus fixed mindset, and rightfully so, it's time that we consider how we can also embody the innovator's mindset to take the growth mindset to a deeper level.

The challenge schools have in cultivating the innovator's mindset is that (traditionally speaking) the focus of education is on the 3Cs: compliance, control, and conformity. Yes, a number of classrooms and schools today emphasize the need to empower learners, but compliance, control, and conformity remain the focus in many educational settings. It's observed everywhere from telling students exactly where to sit, rather than supporting them to identify how they learn best, to assigning work with explicit directions rather than empowering learners to engage in goal setting and selecting how they want to demonstrate their learning.

When education focuses on these 3Cs, the message conveyed to students is that their ideas aren't as valuable as their teachers'. Likewise, it reinforces the belief that rules and expectations of how to learn (based on the individual teacher) hold greater importance than students' individual needs. How can we possibly support our children to develop a genuine appreciation for learning and to actively do something meaningful with the information they acquire if we're not fostering curiosity, empowering student voice, and unleashing creativity within a culture of authentic relationships that encourages them to step beyond their comfort zone as thoughtful risk-takers? The answer is we can't.

Embrace Thinking Differently

The disconnect between school and the world in which our children are growing up leaves students ill prepared for life outside the classroom. In bright contrast to education's slow rate of change are companies such as Uber and Lyft, which offer peer-to-peer ridesharing in answer to the challenges of public transportation. Behind these companies—and so many other innovative companies like them—are creative entrepreneurs who look at problems *differently,* then find ways to revolutionize entire industries. It may very well be a learner sitting in *your* classroom who has the next big idea that will contribute to significant improvements in our world. But that kind of innovation will only come from people who are encouraged to explore ideas, try new things, and to challenge the status quo.

The good news is that children are curious by nature. They're inquisitive explorers, makers, and creators. My question is, do we as educators see and embrace this side of our students? Are we providing ample opportunities for our students to explore? Are we accommodating their unique needs? Do we acknowledge the deep thinkers who ponder life's mysteries and carve out time for them to dig deeper? If we are going to help our learners develop as innovators and world changers, we must tap into their innate curiosity and intentionally craft opportunities for learners to explore, inquire, create, and discover.

My youngest son, Nolan, is insatiably curious and seems to have an extensive list of questions he yearns to explore. He is a fierce negotiator who not only exudes charisma but understands how to leverage it to his personal advantage, which may not always jive with the adults; however, just imagine if teachers consistently recognized these strengths and then supported him in learning how to use them appropriately in the classroom. My eldest, Julian, is passionate about creating storyboards, video production, and editing content. He's quick-witted, perceptive, and is constantly innovating through his creations. With every assignment Julian compliantly completes, I can't help but wonder if he'd be more deeply invested in his learning if permitted to infuse his interests within his work? While both boys exhibit a handful of the qualities admired in adults, they're typically not the qualities we focus on or embrace in schools. Nonetheless, I'm willing to bet that we all agree these qualities are invaluable in life. Their traits are what make them original and, personally, I hope they never diminish as a result of caving to the pressure to conform. Within a fertile environment that places an intentional emphasis on developing the strengths and talents of each individual, the characteristics of an innovator's mindset are nourished to blossom.

The Need for Divergent Thinking

A fascinating study conducted by George Land and Beth Jarman supports the need for shifts in our learning environments. Both Land and Jarman had a desire to better understand the creativity levels of 1,600 children who ranged in ages from three to five years old. Using the same test Land designed for NASA to help identify innovative engineers and scientists, Land and Jarman were curious to see the results when used with young children. As part of a longitudinal study, the test was repeated with the same cohort of children at ages ten and ages fifteen. The results are truly astonishing.

Take a look how children at different ages scored at the genius level on the creative thinking scale:[2]

* Amongst five-year-olds, 98 percent scored at the genius level.
* Amongst ten-year-olds, 30 percent scored at the genius level.
* Amongst fifteen-year-olds, 12 percent scored at the genius level.
* The same test given to 280,000 adults (average age of thirty-one), only 2 percent scored at the genius level.

From this study, many conclude that as our children journey through traditional school systems, their levels of creativity decrease.

In a world where entrepreneurship and innovative advancements are desired and seen as essential to our future, we have to take every measure to ensure that we home in on opportunities to cultivate creative thinking skills in our learners.

In education, we often place emphasis on convergent as opposed to divergent thinking. Divergent thinking promotes the creation of multiple solutions to various problems and is characterized by diverse and creative thought. Convergent thinking, on the other hand, is defined as seeking a single correct answer to a question and is necessary for engaging in critical thinking and being able to analyze problems using information and logic. Although both are critical to the process of learning, fostering divergent thinking promotes the creation of new ideas or unique wonderings. If we place emphasis on finding one right answer by primarily focusing on convergent thinking through frequent multiple-choice assignments, students are eventually influenced to stop considering all of the possibilities. They learn, instead, to focus on mastering specific skills or facts to memorize.

The data of children who scored at the genius level explicitly shows how divergent thinking decreases the older our children grow. We can foster creativity by developing divergent thinking in learners. Land notes that in education, we often engage learners in both convergent and divergent thinking at the same time. The trouble is that children have been taught to come up with new ideas and then to evaluate them immediately. As a result, inside the brain, neurons begin to fight each other as we create an idea but then criticize it. When neurons are conflicted, creative thought stalls.[3]

In our schools, we need to be creating experiences that encourage learners to consider and explore new ideas within a culture where all individuals (educators and students) are supported in developing new ways of thinking, promoting more in-depth learning.

More than ever in today's world, we need to empower learners to explore new possibilities and ideas by fostering divergent thinking, thereby expanding on creativity. Carving out time for learners to ponder their curiosities and explore their wonderings inspires our youth to stretch their thinking to ideate. Following ample time to consider various ideas, learners then benefit from reflecting and retooling their work, which entails convergent thinking.

"Divergent Thinking
Sir Ken Robinson" video

Contributing to Stories by Shaping Mindsets

Finding that picture by Nolan on my coffee table that day sparked a sense of urgency in me. I felt more driven than ever before to challenge mediocrity and stagnant approaches in education. I want schools to draw out all of our children's passions, creativity, and innovative thinking. Let's be honest: no kid is passionate about completing worksheets! Those who may appear to be are often seeking to appease the teacher and have mastered how to be successful at traditional school. We need to address the fact that as educators, we're shaping the mindsets of our students, and our actions contribute to our learners' stories. While we may have mandates to follow and assessments to administer, we have to remember that for the success of our nation in this competitive global market, we must empower learning and create the conditions for students to flourish through authentic experiences.

For the success of our nation in this competitive global market, we must empower learning and create the conditions for students to flourish through authentic experiences.

Countless educators are doing amazing things for kids. I see it in working with many of my colleagues, through my connections with educators in schools I work with, and on social media. They're passionate about growing themselves to create the best experiences and learning environments possible. I'll admit that I don't have all the answers; however, I'm here to inspire conversations around ways we can support one another to ignite a culture of innovation by reimagining schools, fostering divergent thinking, and encouraging originality in our learners. We're all in this together, and we are not meant to walk this journey alone, as the field of education can feel overwhelming if we allow it. Together we can author our future chapters and collectively contribute to the development of our learners' stories by taking the L.E.A.P.

L.E.A.P. is an acronym that illustrates a journey toward continuous growth where we as educators collaboratively work alongside our youth to create empowering learning experiences. The remainder of this book follows that journey.

Take the L.E.A.P.

Part I—Luminous Culture

We'll start with a focus on fostering a culture that shines a light on all individuals' ability to create and allows them a safe space where they can step beyond their comfort zone and innovate. We'll begin by reflecting on our personal stories to identify what has impacted us to be who we are today as educators. From there, we will explore the importance of trust, the impact of leadership, and how we can all contribute to a luminous culture regardless of our role. A culture embedded in authentic relationships, with trust as the cornerstone, serves as the launching point for any successful organization. We'll explore how embracing responsible risk-taking, whether it's a tiny step outside of your comfort zone, a gigantic step, or somewhere in the middle, is a necessary mindset that primes our behaviors for new beginnings.

Part II—Empowered Learning

In Part II, we will embark on a journey to better understand how empowering learning contributes to the creation of a culture of innovation, by encouraging students to be active participants in their education. We'll do this by reimagining learning through incorporating the 6Cs: curiosity, creativity, communication, critical thinking, collaboration, and connectedness. We will identify ways to catalyze empowerment and leverage learners' interests to transform learning experiences.

Part III—Authenticity in Learning

Together we'll explore how we can create authentic learning experiences through harnessing the power of embracing a maker culture, infusing interests and passions in learning, and embedding the elements of project-based learning. Part III is not meant to serve as a how-to manual to be followed step-by-step. It is more of a recipe that contains the vital ingredients to support us on our journey to empower learners to create experiences for themselves. Those ingredients can be mixed in a variety of ways, unique to our learners, to create meaningful experiences. The end result is a lasting impact that compels students to perceive school and learning in a new light. Our goal is to deepen thinking, empower voice, and enhance learning through supporting students as knowledge constructors and designers, thus elevating intrinsic motivation.

Part IV—Potential Soars

When we tap into our unique strengths and empower our students to do the same, we leave a lasting legacy on one another, the school community, and ultimately our most precious commodity: our students. That's when potential truly soars. Jim Rohn, speaker and author, said, "The big challenge is to become all that you have the possibility of becoming. You cannot believe what it does to the human spirit to maximize your human potential and stretch yourself to the limit." Each of us can ignite a movement and support learners and colleagues to continuously move forward with confidence. As education and our world continues to evolve, we need *people who can forge ahead and innovate for the next generation.* As we take this L.E.A.P. together, we can harness our strengths to unleash our individual talent and create the experiences that allow us all to thrive.

When I think back on the day that I found the picture Nolan drew, I can't help but wonder how that scenario could have been different for him. What if he'd been immersed in a culture rich with relationships, empowered as a learner, and had authenticity incorporated in his learning? Fortunately, he has had phenomenal educators since who have done just that, and I'm forever thankful for their dedication. Every child deserves this opportunity, but it shouldn't be in isolation.

Get ready, because we're going to take the L.E.A.P.!

Part I
Luminous Culture

Chapter 1
What's Your Story?

Limitations live only in our minds.
But if we use our imaginations, our
possibilities become limitless.

—Jamie Paolinetti

Our stories *shape* us.

From the most beautiful moments to the most challenging, each has the potential to shape how we view our past, approach new situations, and move forward in life. Those moments combine to create the stories we tell of and about ourselves. They impact how we perceive relationships, the behaviors of others, and even ourselves. Our stories, vast and complex, contribute to who we are as individuals. "Life stories do not simply reflect personality. They are personality, or more accurately, they are important parts of personality, along with other parts, like dispositional traits, goals, and values," writes Dan McAdams, a professor of psychology at Northwestern University, and Erika Manczak, in a chapter for the *APA Handbook of Personality and Social Psychology.*[1]

While some of us may have chapters we would prefer not to reopen, each of us has sections that bestow hope, joy, and inspiration. Reflecting on various chapters within our stories contributes to a better understanding of who we are individually, and even why we do what we do in our individual roles as educators. Hearing others' stories and sharing our own can drive positive transformation and foster empathy and understanding. Thus, as our stories shape us individually, they also allow us to connect, grow, and flourish collectively. Each of us comes from a different path, but in our schools, our stories collide.

Insights from My Story

When I decided to become a teacher, I knew I wanted to create different—*better*–experiences than those of my childhood. Although many of my teachers had a positive influence on me throughout my youth, the number of negative experiences far outweighed the positive.

Many of my teachers wielded fear as a weapon to enforce compliance and used ridicule to ensure we didn't step out of line. And while the majority of teachers were fair, learning often lacked meaning or relevance in my eyes. I always felt that there had to be something more than being assigned work, completing it, and summarizing with an assessment.

I did have some excellent teachers, such as my seventh-grade history teacher, Mr. Merritt. I fondly recall the time he jumped up on his desk and threw a pot on the floor to bring the melting pot alive with a metaphoric visualization. He empowered us to be creative in how we demonstrated our knowledge about the history of radio by selecting any way to share our learning with our peers. To this day, I can still remember how badly my cheeks hurt from laughing as we did numerous takes of a video-recorded radio show dressed as Groucho

Marx. We took immense pride in our project because we had complete ownership over the final product and couldn't wait to present our work to our classmates. Thank you, Mr. Merritt, for bringing the curriculum to life!

These small moments, both positive and negative, shaped my story and helped to cut the path I would travel to become an educator. It was during my years at the State University of Cortland in upstate New York when I explored my interests in psychology. Understanding how the brain learns and the connections to the behaviors of individuals was, and still is, fascinating to me. The more I studied child psychology and neuroscience, the more I felt pulled in the direction of desiring to have a better understanding of how children learn. When I realized the degree to which educators have the potential to shape children's lives by contributing to their story, my perception of education shifted. It was at that point that I began my journey into the field of education with a minor in psychology.

A Rising Opportunity

Working alongside my professors and peers in the Education Department, I saw an opportunity to do something drastically different. My mission became fostering a community where students genuinely enjoy learning and recognize that they're capable of anything that they put their minds to with practice and support from their teachers. Shaking up traditional learning experiences by creating empowering, authentic, and meaningful opportunities felt like a vital part of that mission. From my study in psychology, I understood that teachers have the potential to turn lives around. We can be the difference makers in the lives of children—the influencers who offer positive contributions to the development of their story—and my vision became ensuring that every child had as many positive experiences as possible. With phenomenal professors leading our education courses, my imagination took flight.

One professor stood out above all others as an influencer on my journey: Timothy Slekar, PhD. As an education activist, he captivated my attention by going against the grain of the majority of college professors. Instead of merely having us read books and write essays about what we learned in a course called Foundations of Education, he shared examples depicting protests against standardized testing and exposed us to video recordings to get a glimpse into schools that facilitated testing pep assemblies. In these videos, kids were seen feverishly chanting, "Pass the test," alongside their peers and educators, as if at some sort of hyped-up political rally. As an outsider watching, it felt unsettling that chanting about assessments seemed more of a priority than creating meaningful learning experiences. Through Slekar's instruction, I developed a mindset that fostered my ability to step back and consider why we do what we do in education as well as the effects of our actions. Because of him, I embrace the belief that it's my role as an educator to challenge conventional thinking.

I entered the field of education to be a difference maker, just as I hope most educators do. Due largely to Slekar's influence on me, I felt determined to create phenomenal learning opportunities to support all kids, knowing that what happened in the classroom could start a ripple effect in my students' lives. The road hasn't always been smooth, and I've experienced some difficulty along the way, but my mission remains the same. Nothing will deter me from empowering students instead of empowering learning. And I know I'm not alone in this endeavor.

Looking through a New Lens

Katie Martin, PhD, the head of partnerships-West at AltSchool, didn't have a rosy school experience either. Similar to my own schooling experience, she felt that teachers weren't connecting with students and didn't know who she was as an individual. She enjoyed connecting with friends at school, but academically did only what she needed to get by. While Martin wanted to work with and help people, education wasn't a path she was interested in taking, and she worked diligently to find her way around it. After having the opportunity in college to spend time in classrooms and be with teachers, she recognized that she was starting to find her place. This opportunity helped her to understand what she wanted to do as a teacher herself. Katie Martin went into teaching, not because she loved school but because she wanted to empower students and show them that their voices matter.[2]

In her TEDx Talk, "Teachers Create What They Experience," Martin gives us a glimpse into her story through her experience from third grade. She and her classmates were assigned the book *The Mouse and The Motorcycle*. After reading the book, they had to answer questions about it to prove they had read it. This approach to reading and developing comprehension through accountability measures caused her to hate the book. In her TEDx Talk, Katie Martin says, "I remember thinking, *There's got to be another way. I wish my teacher knew a better way*."

Martin could have easily followed in her predecessors' footsteps by teaching the way she had been taught, but she explains, "I went into teaching because I wanted kids to know that their voices matter, and I want to empower them to understand that they can access the world through new opportunities and learning. And now that I'm a mom, it matters to me more than ever."[3]

Martin's story resonates with me on a personal and professional level. As teachers, we must examine whether our instruction is sparking enthusiasm to learn or slowly diminishing the flame. Sure, it may feel easier to give learners questions to respond to, but empowering them to create their own questions based on their wonderings is significantly more powerful. Teachers may opt to do as Martin's teacher did because it is how they were taught or because it's a method that models what students see on standardized assessments. Together, we will explore ways to infuse alternative approaches that are authentic, and therefore more meaningful. In her book, *Learner-Centered Innovation*, Martin discusses the fact that we tend to replicate the ingrained paradigms from own experiences. That truth is the reason she focuses today on helping educators become change agents who bring student-centered learning to the forefront.

Refocus Your Story

Wade King, director of curriculum and instruction at The Ron Clark Academy, and coauthor of *The Wild Card*, shares his story of enduring a very challenging childhood in which he experienced abuse and homelessness. He recalls having to sleep on couches at friends' houses or on park benches when things were at their worst. With school being the only constant in his life, he attended daily because he had no other place to go. King reflects, "I needed teachers to push me, and I'm grateful now that they did."[4]

Although King enjoyed going to school and loved his teachers, he found that he often had to identify ways to motivate himself. He'd arrive at school and think, *Okay, I'm going to go in here and pretend this is Mission Impossible.*

I wonder how many students are enacting situations like this to maintain focus or to motivate themselves to learn. As teachers, we can create experiences that empower students and enhance learning in ways that influence them to develop motivation. Today, King does just that by designing phenomenal learning opportunities for students that allow his childhood motivational tactics to come into play for all kids.[5]

King's life could have taken a very different path, but he chose to go into teaching to give other kids what his teachers gave him: love and hope. With that mission in mind, he found the drive to embrace this challenging career. In a #KidsDeserveIt podcast episode, King shares that love is a good place to start, but you need a purpose that will help you stick when times are challenging. With passion, King states, "I hope all teachers love kids, but that's not enough." He then questions, "Why do you love kids? A lot of us who are a part of education wake up when it's dark outside, and most of us go home when it's still dark outside, or about to be dark outside. Why do you care for kids? What is your purpose of really doing this?"

We must be cognizant of how our experiences—both positive and negative—shape our stories. It is important to remain aware that the same is true for every one of our colleagues and students. Because our stories shape the way we view life, people from different backgrounds may view the same event in very different ways—which impact the ways we relate to one another and the paths we choose to take. Our job as educators is to ensure that the moments we share with students and the kind of learning experiences we provide impact them in such a way that drives them to personal and academic success.

L.E.A.P. Onward

Understanding our stories and how personal experiences influence our journeys as educators allows us to honor the positive impact others have had on us, while using the negative experiences as fuel to create better experiences. Likewise, seeking to understand the stories of others fosters compassion and empathy, contributing to a luminous culture. After reflecting on our backstory, we can move forward as we explore how we can author our future stories for the betterment of ourselves and our learners. Together, we'll shatter the status quo of learning as we take the L.E.A.P. and bring the very best experiences to learners.

L.E.A.P. Tips and Takeaways

* Each of us has a unique story that contributes to who we are as an educator; leverage what ignites passion in you.
* Placing ourselves in the shoes of our learners and reflecting on moments of our own schooling provide us with valuable insights on how we can create the conditions and experiences to empower learning.

L.E.A.P. beyond Your Boundaries

Share your reflections, questions, and ideas using #LEAPeffect.

1. What experiences have influenced you to be the teacher you are today?
2. Who has been a positive force of influence on you?
3. In what ways have they impacted you and your approach to education?

Chapter 2
Take the High Ropes

The hardest part of learning something
new is not embracing new ideas, but
letting go of old ones.

—Todd Rose,
Author of *The End of Average*

Suspended seventy-feet or three stories high in the air, balancing on a steel cable, I began to wobble unsteadily. As the adrenaline kicked in, numbness found its way from the tips of my fingers to my elbows. I tightly gripped the bristly rope that ran along my side and stood in place, utterly motionless, until I could regain the confidence with which I had begun the ropes course. While I recouped, a blur caught my attention. Upon second glance, I recognized the blur as our youngest son, Nolan, whizzing by on the obstacle beside me. I watched as Nolan leapt from challenge to challenge without skipping a beat. Seeing him caused my heart to race even faster. If his foot missed the anticipated placement, he laughed with glee and just moved forward. In fact, there were times he lifted both feet dangling, then called out, "Look, Mom! No hands!"

Nolan felt 100 percent secure, which allowed him to advance as a carefree risk-taker. While I had started on the lower ropes section at the course, he went straight to the challenges on the high ropes.

Let's rewind to the moments before setting foot on the ropes course. When we arrived, the guides demonstrated that we were securely harnessed. To ensure we grasped the magnitude of our safety, they showed how they could hang safely by lifting their feet without falling to their demise. Nolan trusted the ropes. With absolutely no fear, he flourished in his ability to take risks.

Turning my attention to our eldest, Julian, I observed him navigating the course with a reasonable level of caution. He didn't appear fearful, but his natural tendency is to know all the nuts and bolts of a challenge before taking the first step. He's very thoughtful in his actions, which serves him well in life. Julian wasn't hesitant, but more evaluative of his approach to each challenge and seemed to be enjoying the thrill of the experience as he was simultaneously excited and deep in concentration.

Venture Elicits Varying Responses

As I continued scanning the ropes course, I saw individuals with varying abilities move forward at their own pace while guides in the vicinity checked in, continuously demonstrating safety and promoting confidence in those on the course. Feeling a level of safety allowed each individual to take reasonable risks and navigate the course with growing confidence; however, I noticed that every so often, someone would retreat to safety and choose not to proceed after attempting to step out on the course.

What happens in schools isn't unlike what happened on that ropes course. While some of us avidly advance as innovators, striving to motivate and challenge colleagues to try new ideas, others want to know every minute detail and speculate all of the possibilities to grasp the big picture and purpose before committing to taking action. Our schools benefit from both types of personalities: We need to think critically about what we're working toward, and we also want to move forward at a steady pace, creating deeply meaningful learning experiences.

Just as certain individuals turned back to safety after stepping out on the ropes course, our colleagues may appear to be unwilling to leave their zone of comfort. We may like the safety and familiarity of the way we've always done things. For example, on the ropes course, individuals felt the very real physiological effects associated with a fear of heights, and it's likely that some educators who fear change may experience similar emotions. But I'd like to challenge the notion that just because someone appears to be unwilling to change, they are fans of the status quo club. It's entirely possible that those of us who fear change or are uncomfortable with it simply require more support, encouragement, or time to process along the way. Perhaps some individuals aren't certain *why* it's crucial to step forward. Likewise, it's equally as important that we listen to the perspectives of everyone we work alongside. Each individual has valuable insights that will help us ensure we have covered all our bases.

It is essential to be in tune with our needs and those of our colleagues within our organizations if we are going to successfully decipher what drives each of us and how we can support one another to move forward. Although many view this as an administrative duty, we all play a fundamental role in not just creating but sustaining shifts that are essential to support our youth to be future ready. As teachers, we are the ones who are directly creating experiences and opportunities that will guide students to empower learning for themselves. In fact, we'll gain momentum quicker and see gains faster if shifts are led by teachers as opposed to solely administrators.

Understanding what our colleagues require allows us to be more intentional in our approach to feel supported as we take new risks. Sometimes it's a matter of helping others to understand that it is okay to make mistakes as long as we are reflecting, learning, and refining our work. Let's face it, those of us who have taken various risks have likely failed numerous times only to get back up and persevere, learning from each experience. Reflecting on failure leads us to retool, thus fostering innovative learning opportunities for students. Teachers who have taken the L.E.A.P. do not possess some superhuman power, but rather they too are subject to failure; it's how they move forward toward growth that sets them apart.

What's Your Why?

While we can each take the L.E.A.P. independently, we benefit even more when we join hands and support one another as we navigate our collective journey. At the same time, it's important to remember that it's okay if your journey looks different from someone else's. In our field, we need to aspire to empower ourselves and fellow educators to be significant agents of change regardless of the starting point. We can do this by identifying our *why*.

Recognizing what influenced you to go into education or reflecting on the reason you're seeking to take the L.E.A.P. may serve as your why. In *Start With Why: How Great Leaders Inspire Everyone to Take Action*, author Simon Sinek shares the concept of the Golden Circle. The Golden Circle demonstrates the importance of starting with why you're interested in doing something, explaining the *how*, and then describing what it is or entails. Utilizing the concept of the Golden

Cultivating and sustaining a culture of innovation requires a delicate balance. When we recognize educators who are ready to take on new challenges, we need to provide encouragement along with the space to take off, but not in isolation. Within every district, some educators are comfortable taking on new ventures, while others require time to adjust. Honoring and celebrating individual qualities creates a safety net where educators trust they're supported when it's their time to L.E.A.P. onward. Likewise, when we sense educators are uncomfortable about shifts, we need to be cognizant of the environment they're in and who they are connected with, then nurture the culture to support their growth. Oftentimes, teachers voice that they feel overloaded with initiatives. Having a narrower focus and creating solutions for the barriers of initiative success—i.e., lack of time, initiative fatigue, mental capacity, etc.—is crucial in supporting teachers to embrace shifts. In fact, coauthors of *Learning Transformed*, Tom Murray and Eric Sheninger, claim, "As school leaders work to redesign their schools, they must be careful not to immerse themselves, their teams, and their students in an alphabet soup of initiatives. In our experience, initiative overload is one of the primary reasons that transformational change fails."[1] It's important that we are mindful of our approach, and advance collectively.

Circle relates to education because we are more likely to feel driven to devote time and effort when we not only understand the why but passionately believe in the why. For example, if I am interested in encouraging colleagues to partner with me on infusing project-based learning (PBL) into the school year, I would start with why:

PBL engages students in deep and meaningful learning experiences that can be transformative. Rather than learners completing assignments directed by the teacher, they develop their own driving questions and begin to recognize how school connects to life beyond the classroom walls, inspiring students to be driven to learn while building future-ready skills.

Following the why, we would collaboratively brainstorm the how and what that best fits individual teams and students. If we start by just sharing what we are doing, meaning and purpose is lacking.

Identifying our why and sharing it can evoke passion in one another. As a result, individuals contribute more and feel compelled to venture forward, thereby inspiring a culture where learners are empowered to explore, create, and innovate.

Evoking passion is not the sole responsibility of administrators, rather it's something we can all contribute to. Sinek explains that if we want individuals to be invested in leaving the organization better than they found it, we must evoke passion. Sinek claims:

> Passion comes from feeling like you are a part of something that you believe in, something bigger than yourself. If people do not trust that a company is organized to advance the why, then the passion is diluted. Without managed trust, people will show up to do their jobs and they will worry primarily about themselves.[2]

When passionate about your why, gain momentum by involving others. Reach out to a few colleagues to see who is interested in collaborating on the new idea together.

In today's world, we need committed educators to spark wonder and awe while encouraging the spark to spread contagiously as
students continue to inquire, seek answers, and develop new questions around relevant topics. The data shared by the World Economic
Forum's *Future of Jobs Report* demonstrates *why we need to embrace
the concept of thinking differently about education.* Take a look at the
anticipated shift in the ten essential job skills in just seven years' time.
From 2015 to 2022, creativity climbs, and critical thinking remains
consistent, while quality control—a skill focused on repetition and
compliance—falls completely off the list.

2022 Skills Outlook, World Economic Forum
Top Ten Skills

2022	2015
1. Analytical thinking and innovation	1. Complex problem solving
2. Active learning and learning strategies	2. Coordinating with others
3. Creativity, originality and initiative	3. People management
4. Technology design and programing	4. Critical thinking
5. Critical thinking and analysis	5. Negotiation
6. Complex problem-solving	6. Quality control
7. Leadership and social influence	7. Service orientation
8. Emotional intelligence	8. Judgment and decision-making
9. Reasoning, problem-solving and ideation	9. Active listening
10. Systems analysis and evaluation	10. Creativity

Readily, we can see the need to be crafting learning opportunities that empower students as complex problem solvers and critical thinkers while striving to place an intentional emphasis on creativity in the classroom. According to Lee Crockett, author and speaker, "No pupil in the history of education is like today's modern learner. This is a complex, energetic, and tech-savvy individual."[3]

By fostering a robust culture that embraces change, we can begin to step forward to consistently provide learners with the experiences they need to develop the skills required in today's world and their future. When a school's culture has trust as the cornerstone, educators feel supported to take risks to grow and respectfully challenge one another to push thinking, thus creating the conditions to support learners as responsible risk-takers too.

Trust Elevates Our Ability to Venture Forward

Educators in all roles require support. If our goal is to increase innovative practices and opportunities for our students, we need to take a step back and analyze how we're nurturing the culture. An educator in my professional learning network shared with me he had been a risk-taker but stepped back into the safe zone when trust diminished between him and his building principal. Let's explore and learn from his story.

An educator I was connected with for years via social media (let's call him Matthew) spread his wings early in his career, largely in part to having unwavering support from administrators he worked alongside. Over the course of twelve years, he continued to L.E.A.P. and truly soared. With numerous accolades, including awards at the local, state, and national level, he demonstrated a keen understanding of pedagogy and innovative practices that empowered learning. Matthew built on his repertoire year after year to strengthen learning experiences for students. No stranger to incorporating robotics and coding into the curriculum, he leveraged technology to empower voice, choice, and accelerate learning. Furthermore, he served as a teacher leader, enthusiastically supporting his colleagues. Matthew valued the importance of encouraging individuals to move beyond their zone of comfort through cultivating trust. He recognized that such encouragement has the potential to impact the most important members of our schools: our learners.

Matthew and his building principal were close as colleagues, and they shared a similar philosophy of education. The more Matthew's career blossomed, however, the more strained their relationship became. From Matthew's perspective, it seemed that his principal resented his achievements. His principal never once celebrated his accomplishments in a staff meeting, let alone an email or newsletter. Instead, his demeanor toward Matthew was cavalier, and he would even strike Matthew with snarky remarks at unexpected times. Matthew began to feel that his vast efforts were unappreciated, and it hurt. As a result, Matthew, who cared deeply about his school community and about pushing the boundaries to cultivate innovative practices, began to pull back from his relationship with his principal. As a teacher leader, he knew that if the roles were reversed, he would want to celebrate the accomplishments of colleagues.

If what you are doing is important, you will encounter resistance. If what you are doing isn't important, it will be easy.

—Donald Miller

Over time, Matthew and his principal went from a collaborative relationship, discussing how to cultivate change and empower learners, to a relationship where hierarchical decision-making reigned and dishonesty from his principal ensued. This new territory left Matthew feeling unsteady navigating the high ropes. Perhaps Matthew's principal felt professional jealousy and wanted to push him out of the school.

While there's much more to this story, and regardless of the reasons the relationship soured, the outcome was that Matthew's colleagues and school community ultimately lost out when he decided to pull back and retreat to the safe zone of the status quo in some areas of his career. Being the dedicated educator he is, Matthew continued navigating the high ropes where he felt confident by creating dynamic learning opportunities for students in the classroom and supporting the team of teachers that he worked alongside. But he stepped down to the low ropes by pulling back from committees and away from collaborative partnerships with his principal as a result of feeling cast aside.

Situations such as Matthew's are rarely discussed, and they occur far too often. I challenge administrators and teachers alike to reflect upon how others' successes make you feel. Do you celebrate the accomplishments of colleagues or feel threatened by their growth? Truly knowing the answer to this question can help move you past fixed mindset denial and serve as a pivotal step toward cultivating a synergistic school culture. Likewise, we must encourage one another to take the high ropes by fostering a culture where everyone feels genuinely valued. To do that, we have to work through these challenging scenarios with patience and professionalism, realizing that everyone's actions either positively or negatively impact the culture. When we step into the shoes of individuals in our organization and learn their stories, we can begin to understand their perspective and how it shapes their behavior.

If you are in a situation similar to this, consider one or a combination of the following to move forward:

1. Examine your own role in the situation. Is it possible that there's something you did to contribute?
2. Engage in a crucial conversation by leading with questions rather than blaming. For example, ask, "Can you help me understand..." or "I would appreciate your perspective on..."
3. Remain focused on solutions, not on casting blame. Be prepared to provide suggestions for resolution.
4. Every experience is a lesson; reflect on what you can learn from it. My experiences have influenced how I interact with others and lead as a result. I've learned what not to do just as much as I've learned what to do.
5. If all else fails, it's okay to give yourself permission to look for healthier career options in education. While I believe in working toward a common solution, there may be a situation in which you'd be better off finding a school that is a better fit.

By actively working to be part of the solution, we can play a pivotal role in contributing to a supportive culture. If our ultimate goal is to ignite a culture of innovation, we must first lay the foundation for individuals to step forward in trust.

Lead to L.E.A.P.

In speaking with a select group of teachers at the 2017 ISTE conference on the topics of leadership and bringing innovative experiences to learners, I learned how different schools approached change. Interestingly, while we all shared that we seek to bring innovative practices to the classroom, some of the teachers told me they were called upon to share during professional learning sessions and peer observations while others expressed that they felt their voices weren't heard or respected. One teacher expressed that she felt the only way she would manage to create the shifts she envisioned in education beyond her own classroom would be to take an administrative position!

I hold a deep respect for the work administrators do, but as a teacher leader, I believe *every* individual should be encouraged to embrace his or her inner leader. Leadership—at every level—is a must. If our goal is to move our schools forward, creating a culture of innovation, we cannot follow a top-down model. Let's explore.

Administrative roles carry the expectation of leadership, but any educator can step up as a leader. In my experience, teacher leadership can be powerful, particularly when the culture supports it. Leadership isn't about management; it is about influence, adding value, and supporting and encouraging others' growth. In *Culturize,* educational leader and author Jimmy Casas shares his view on leadership:

> You don't have to have a leadership title to be a leader. You just have to lead. When you have a disposition about you that others immediately recognize and sometimes want to emulate, you are a leader. When you draw people in and make them want to be around you, you are a leader. Maybe you have a unique skill set that people quickly notice and appreciate, or maybe it's your words or tendency to notice the best in others that inspires the people around you to want to be better.[4]

All too frequently, teachers wait to be empowered by their principal. Without a clear path, we may feel uncertain about how to engage as a teacher leader. In some cases, teacher leaders feel the support of their colleagues, and, unfortunately, there are also times in which we may feel isolated. Isolation can trigger more uncertainty and leave even the strongest teachers feeling unsupported or fearful about stepping outside their comfort zones. This is why it's critical that we foster a culture of collaborative leadership, rooted in trust, where each individual champions the notion that they, too, are a leader.

Here are four ways to foster a culture of collaborative leadership, whatever your current role:

1. **Add value to those who work alongside you.** Keep in mind that sometimes it's administrators who hear the least amount of positive feedback regarding their efforts. Acknowledging the work and efforts of others, big and small, can go a long way to building confidence.

2. **Remain cognizant of the shared vision of your school and district.** Engage in collaborative conversations with fellow colleagues to identify how you can all progress toward that vision, and then act on it. Recognize areas where you can provide support and be willing to seek help when necessary.

3. **Establish trust with administrators and colleagues.** Participate in co-planning, share resources, and be dependable by consistently following through with your efforts. Nurture relationships and connect by engaging in conversations on common interests.

4. **Involve a variety of community stakeholders to foster a positive school culture and carry the shared vision forward.** Inviting stakeholders to share their voice and contribute to the vision develops a mutual understanding that we can all contribute to the betterment of the school community and learning experiences for our youth.

When administrators and teachers take the time to get to know their colleagues and one another's areas of strength—and then make those areas known—everyone feels like they can be successful.

Celebrating a diversity of skills and talents makes everyone feel capable of contributing to the efforts of the school.

Our Learners Need Us to Venture Forward

Each school comprises a unique community of learners. We can honor our learners by reimagining education and creating experiences that foster autonomy through taking the L.E.A.P. As educators, *we* have the potential to create amazing opportunities in our schools by empowering learning. As we step out on the high ropes, remember that we will need to demonstrate tenacity and believe that together we can create the experiences we imagine for learners. In *The End of Average,* Todd Rose shares his own compelling story. As I read his book, I couldn't help but wonder more about the experiences that he faced throughout his childhood.

Rose reflects, "Every time I attempted something, it would end up in failure." At the age of eighteen, Rose dropped out of high school with a 0.9 GPA. He attempted to hold down minimum-wage jobs in an effort to support his wife and two sons. Rose recalls, "Almost everyone said the problem was me. That I was lazy, stupid, or most frequently a troublemaker. More than one school official told my parents that they would have to temper their expectations of what I'd be able to achieve in life. But even during my lowest moments, I always felt that something wasn't right with this analysis. I felt sure I had something to offer. It just seemed like there was a profound mismatch between who I really was and the way the world saw me. Eventually, I stopped trying to conform to the system and instead focused on figuring out how to make the system fit to me. It worked. Fifteen years after I dropped out of high school, I was on the faculty at the Harvard Graduate School of Education, where I am now the director of the Mind, Brain, and Education Program."[5]

According to Rose's research, "average" simply doesn't exist, despite the fact that individuals, businesses, and our education system continue to place an emphasis on them. From standardized assessments to data screenings, we're always noting where individuals are. Rose explains that this one-size-fits-all model is contradictory to the notion that we are all individuals with unique strengths that vary. Let's make certain that our youth don't simply feel like they have something to offer; let's help them to discover *what* they have to offer by providing opportunities to explore interests, tapping into their individual strengths and unleashing their potential as contributors to our world. Likewise, as educators, we must allow this for ourselves, too. There is no average teacher; we are all capable and growing at different rates. Let's join hands and continue the collective journey to ensure all, including our learners, are encouraged to take the high ropes.

L.E.A.P. Onward

We know that we need to incorporate learning standards in the classroom and that our students require all of the basics to develop a deeper understanding, but traditional education alone is *not* supporting students to excel in today's world. While some students are receiving outstanding grades, others are falling through the cracks. As educators, we must challenge ourselves to reflect on *why* we're doing what we're doing. Let's carefully consider whether we are truly inspiring and empowering learners to reach their full potential. Together, we have what it takes as trailblazers who are willing to take the L.E.A.P. and create school cultures where students, teachers, and administrators feel confident enough to risk the high ropes.

L.E.A.P. Tips and Takeaways

* Fostering trust builds a strong foundation to L.E.A.P.
* In cultures that focus on celebrating the accomplishments of individuals, people feel of value and develop the motivation to continue putting forth their best.
* Despite the adversity we face, we own our reactions. We can opt to move forward toward growth—even when we perceive that others are trying to pull us down.
* We need to engage in courageous conversations in a respectful manner to maintain relationships for a healthy culture.

L.E.A.P. beyond Your Boundaries

Share your reflections, questions, and ideas using #LEAPeffect.

1. In talking about risk-taking, what helps you to feel supported and what holds you back?
2. How can you inspire others to take the high ropes?
3. In thinking about Todd Rose's story, how does it connect to the learners that are with you each day?

Chapter 3

Power of Relationships

If we want meaningful change, we have to make a connection to the heart before we can make a connection to the mind.

—George Couros

Kids don't put forth their best effort for people they don't know, like, or trust. To flourish, they need an environment in which they feel safe—a place where they feel cared for and connected. Board certified neurologist and educator, Dr. Judy Willis, describes the important link between student comfort and learning this way: "Comfort level, such as self-confidence, trust, and positive feelings for teachers, and supportive classroom and school communities, are directly related to the state of mind that is compatible with the most successful learning, remembering, and higher order thinking."[1]

Brain-based research supports the notion that if our schools or classrooms are perceived to be intimidating in any way, students will not learn to their highest potential level. Perceived threats send learners into a fight, flight, or freeze mode, which prohibits information from going into long-term memory. Positive, authentic relationships between us and our students—as well as peer-to-peer relationships—help to foster a fertile learning environment where new ideas are encouraged to germinate and abilities, intelligence, talents, and tenacity grow. It is in this kind of culture that children and teens develop an innovator's mindset.

Every Child Has a Story

Each student comes to us with his or her own unique story, and every child has potential waiting to be discovered. Sometimes it's simple to identify learners' strengths. Those who have excelled socially, emotionally, and academically throughout their school career stand out and are often easy to connect with on a relational level. For others, it's easier to identify areas of weakness. Those students who exhibit challenging behaviors may disrupt the classroom and even bristle when you try to connect. Their behavior may stem from lack of support or safety in the home, health struggles, or negative experiences in school. Or, like Steve Jobs or Richard Branson, they simply may not have found where their unique skills and talents fit. Branson has admitted that he wasn't a perfect student, saying, "I constantly pushed against rules and authority, and I liked to challenge the way that things were 'always' done. My curiosity often got me into trouble with teachers."[2] Even kids like Branson, who test authority and question *everything*, deserve our support. I believe that as educators it is our moral imperative to encourage all learners in their journey, and relationships are the key to opening the door leading to infinite possibilities.

Oddly enough, the romantic comedy, *How to Lose a Guy in 10 Days*, makes me think about interactions with students who push back on us and how we go about fostering meaningful relationships with them. Now, you may not be a fan of romantic comedies, but for the sake of using it as an example, bear with me! In the movie, Andie Anderson (played by Kate Hudson) works as a resident writer for the "How-To" section for *Composure* magazine. She decides to write an article on "How to Lose a Guy in 10 Days." Her idea is to start dating a guy and then do everything in her power to drive him away. The twist is that Benjamin Barry (played by Matthew McConaughey) was simultaneously dared to prove that he could make a girl fall in love with him. Andie and Benjamin cross paths and become the victims of each other's plans. Andie entertains the audience as she does everything possible to push Benjamin away while he demonstrates relentless admiration to her face. Behind the scenes, he's utterly flabbergasted by her but refuses to give up the challenge of making her fall in love with him.

It's a scenario similar to those we face with children who lack trust. Each year, we head into the new school year already having heard the rumors about "those" kids. No matter how much we attempt to avoid this transfer of information/gossip in hopes of giving students a fresh start each year, it seems inevitable. We end up hearing something that may tempt us to limit the way we think about certain students or hold preconceived ideas about them.

Unlike the situation in *How to Lose a Guy in 10 Days*, Children do not intentionally set out with an agenda to sabotage the relationship between themselves and their teachers. Those who lack trust, however, may push harder on adults to test their love limits. Like the unrelenting Benjamin Barry, we must demonstrate strength, compassion, and empathy and maintain the energy to give our best, day after day—especially when students exhibit challenging behaviors. When you show authentic and unconditional acceptance for even the most fearful or distrusting students, defensive energy will lessen.

It's possible that you have found yourself frustrated and even responded to a child in a way you wish you could take back. The good news is that *each day* is a new opportunity to get back on track. It's important to reflect, retool, and strive to put our best self out there for kids. By investing in relationships, we gain the respect of learners and their families.

Believe in Every Child

Several years ago, I encountered one of the most challenging situations regarding cultivating a relationship with a child in all my years of teaching. On the first day of school, I greeted a girl (I'll call Marie) just as I did all the others. With my knees bent to be at eye level, I held out my hand to shake hers and greet Marie by name. Marie, just nine years old, looked me dead straight in my eyes. With slightly lowered eyelids and dark circles under her eyes, she appeared to be less than impressed with me. Marie let out a deep sigh and slumped her shoulders, refusing to shake my hand. Her eyes drifted to the floor, and she walked past me in an apathetic manner. Of course, having already heard her story, I was determined that this school year would be a blank canvas for her to paint her masterpiece.

All school year, Marie challenged my love limits, testing if I'd give up on her. She employed a variety of tactics from doing the opposite of what was requested, to behaviors that completely sabotaged collaborative teamwork. Marie made gradual progress in all areas, but would often regress following breaks, as kids frequently do. While her peers viewed her as being less capable, I knew that through relationship I could support her in identifying her strengths to flourish.

Throughout the fall, Marie gradually revealed a strong interest and ability in art. Unfortunately, her artistry frequently came out as an avoidance technique; she'd engage herself in drawing as opposed to what other learners were doing. The natural tendency is to demand students comply with the expectations, so I could have easily viewed her behavior of drawing at her discretion as a show of disrespect toward me or her classmates. Knowing that power struggles aren't helpful, I had to get creative to meet her and leverage her interest and talent to both of our advantages. I provided greater choice and began integrating various forms of art, including comics and graphics, to empower all learners to communicate their thinking and learning.

Marie's oppositional behavior began to shift; even better, she pushed the envelope when it came to designing graphics and using coding to create cartoons to depict learning. Tapping into her strengths and empowering choice encouraged Marie to lower her walls. As a result, relationships between peers began to strengthen; she developed greater confidence as her classmates came to her to learn how to code or create a cartoon of characters explaining mathematical processes. Those relationships led to Marie becoming less oppositional and more eager to participate and contribute in class.

On the last day of school, the same girl who wouldn't shake my hand on the first day hugged me with all her might before stepping onto her bus. It brought me to tears. We can never underestimate the impact we have on individuals. I share this story with you because we've all had a "Marie," or will have one at some point. Our impact is far-reaching, and it's our choice how we will affect each child and contribute to their story. Quite honestly, throughout the school year, I often felt like Benjamin from *How to Lose a Guy in 10 Days* but knew it wasn't the case. Relationships are the heartbeat of every successful school, and every child deserves opportunities to flourish, developing their potential.

Foster Deep Connections, Reach the Heart

When learners arrive at my classroom, I greet them with a smile and conversation while upbeat music plays in the background. As we get to know one another, I ask about their hobbies and family members; throughout the day, I carve out time to work one-on-one with learners who require greater support academically, those who require enrichment, and learners who simply benefit from the boost of confidence from encouragement. These simple steps are a good start and allow me to spark relationships with my learners. Fostering deep, authentic connections, however, requires that strategic effort. I've found three specific strategies to be helpful in creating the kind of relationships that move kids and shape their mindsets to ripen them for innovative thinking and learning:

* Being vulnerable and relatable
* Connecting through experiences
* Listening to and validating feelings

1. Be Vulnerable and Relatable

Learners often view teachers as the "experts." I'll be the first to admit I'm not an expert, and I certainly do not know everything. I'm entirely comfortable in expressing this to my learners in part because I've learned that students respect me more when I allow them to see my imperfections.

As a child, I struggled to grasp math concepts. I felt so embarrassed when my teacher called on me because I was unsure whether I had the correct answer. Because of my own experiences, I can relate to how learners want to be viewed as capable, and, more importantly, they want their peers to see them as a valued member of the classroom. Breaking down the walls of fear that surround our students allows them to contribute at a high level regardless of where they are in their learning journey. As a child, I recall holding back due to fearing I would be incorrect in my response. Sharing our vulnerabilities, ones that connect with students' lives, makes us relatable.

In her book *Mathematical Mindsets*, Jo Boaler, PhD, explains a study that demonstrates that the brain grows with each mistake. According to the study, with each error, the mind sparks and develops even if we don't recognize that we made a mistake. The reasoning behind the growth is the catalyst of experiencing challenge. To further support the significance of nurturing the growth mindset in learners, Boaler explains that the study also showed that individuals who embrace the growth mindset were more attentive to errors and therefore had increased brain activity than those who had a fixed mindset.[3] She notes, "If we believe we can learn, and that mistakes are valuable, our brains grow to a greater extent when we make a mistake. This result is highly significant, telling us again how important it is for all of us to believe in ourselves, particularly when we approach something challenging."

My learners became enthralled with the concept that their brain grew with each mistake and that if they embraced a growth mindset, it increased their awareness of errors, leading to more significant improvement. As a result, learners decided that they wanted to share out and celebrate when they made mistakes and the learning that accompanied, leading toward growth.

Through this, learners became more cognizant of their work and eager to identify errors to grasp what occurred. Now, throughout the day, I observe students confidently sharing out their learning and growth through identifying errors. Other times, learners recognize that they have made a mistake and then request input from peers. By being vulnerable, everyone relates a bit better. We have created an open culture where trusting relationships encourage each of us to acknowledge the fact that we're continuously growing.

If we want to inspire our students to engage in learning that leads to divergent thinking, we have to liberate them from fear of making mistakes and encourage them to become responsible risk-takers. You can get the ball rolling by sharing with your students some of the mistakes you have made and how you have learned from them, and most importantly how you have overcome challenges through perseverance. Doing so will help foster trusting relationships with them. Emphasize the importance of persevering when faced with challenges, identifying errors, and applying the learning from mistakes—because that is how we increase our potential to improve.

2. Connect with Kids

Each day, I connect with students by greeting them at the door. From there, we ensure the day begins on a positive note by holding a morning meeting. More specifically, we hold a Responsive Classroom Morning Meeting, an idea I've adapted from the Responsive Classroom.® The organization defines this meeting on their site this way:

"A Responsive Classroom Morning Meeting is an engaging way to start each day, build a strong sense of community, and set children up for success socially and academically. Each morning, students and teachers gather together in a circle for twenty to thirty minutes and interact with one another during four purposeful components:"[4]

In general, I follow the structure detailed below, but many times we make adjustments to fit the unique needs of the learners in our classroom. Often, our group activity incorporates what we're doing within maker education or ties back to students' interests as a way to connect with learners.

1. **Greeting**—Students and teachers greet one other by name.

2. **Sharing**—Students share information about important events in their lives. Listeners often offer empathetic comments or ask clarifying questions.
3. **Group Activity**—Everyone participates in a brief, lively activity that fosters group cohesion and helps students practice social and academic skills (for example, sharing a creation, topics of interest, team-building, etc.)
4. **Morning Message**—Students read and interact with a short message written by their teacher. The message is crafted to help students focus on the work they'll do in school that day.

Regardless of the age you work with, every learner benefits from kicking off the day engaged in relaxed conversations and activities facilitated in a morning meeting (elementary) or class discussions (secondary). It's an ideal way to connect with kids and cultivate relationships amongst all learners.

Connecting with learners by simply being yourself allows kids to see you as relatable and approachable. Danny Steele, a principal, learned that his ultimate passion is connecting with kids. When he was a high school teacher, Steele recalls being silly and genuine were the most effective ways to relate with kids. And even in an administrative role he says, "I've never taken myself too seriously. A lot of adults are patronizing and condescending to kids and talk down to them. One of the best ways to win over kids is not to treat them like kids. Kids gravitate toward that. Sometimes students will sort of mock a teacher or imitate them, and I've seen teachers get so bent out of shape over that and offended, and viewed it as disrespectful. And I would just laugh at the kids and the fact that they saw me laughing at myself and not taking myself too seriously; you know, I think they appreciated that."

To foster deeper connections as a classroom teacher, Steele went out of his way to play pickup basketball with his students and even invited them to have pizza together outside of school, fostering community. Connecting beyond the walls of our schools makes it evident that our efforts are authentic.

> With all of the advances in technology, there are numerous ways in which we can communicate with our learners. For example, third-grade teacher Meg Cernaro used Flipgrid to engage with her students on a snow day. Cernaro is shown in video enthusiastically reading *P is for PIRATE: Inspirational ABCs for Educators*, authored by Dave and Shelley Burgess. Cernaro invites students to respond back by sharing the following:
>
> What are you reading or learning about or doing that's fun on this snow day?
>
> While at home, students had the opportunity to listen to their teacher read and were empowered to create their own video in return to share with their teacher and classmates on how they were spending their snow day. Flipgrid is just one of many tools, and technology will continue to evolve. Tools such as Google Classroom also serve as a platform to connect and communicate. It's important to keep in mind that when selecting tools, we need to identify what's most relevant, engaging, and meaningful to our learners.

3. Listen and Validate Feelings

In the busyness of our days, it's far too easy to get caught up in our agenda. Bells and time blocks often dictate our schedule, and in some cases, scripted curriculum mandates that we stay on pace with others. Constraints will always exist, but if we want learners to excel, we must innovate inside the box, creating time to listen to students and validate their feelings. Lead Learner, Bethany Hill, emphasizes the importance of listening in her blog post, "Let's Take a Walk and Talk About It." Hill points out that kids come to school carrying emotions from home. With this, we've returned to the idea that we all bring our unique stories and experiences with us. The difference is that children, regardless of what age they're at, don't always grasp how to emote in a socially acceptable manner. Learners may exhibit behaviors that cause them to appear apathetic, angry, scared, overly silly, etc. We have to remind ourselves that it is not personal.

In her blog post, Hill reflects on a challenging situation when a child had a behavioral outburst. Upon entering the classroom, the child hid under the table. While each circumstance requires a unique approach, in this case, Hill provided time for the child to calm down. Once calm, the child reached out and said, "Mrs. Hill, I'm ready to go for a walk and talk about it." Hill writes:

> We walked in silence for a few moments, but soon began talking about what frustrated him in the first place. It was all 'stuff' he had brought to school with him . . . frustration from his other environment. The 'stuff' consumed him to a point that he began to blurt out in class and was confrontational with the teacher. We discussed how it is important for him to feel safe, but also for others to feel safe. We connected his actions to the safety of his classroom. He immediately made the connection to why his outbursts disturbed the safe feeling of his classroom.[5]

Hill's responsive approach had an effect not only on the individual child but also on the entire classroom. All of our children deserve to feel supported and safe. The strategy of walking and talking fosters a caring community where individuals feel validated, rather than threatened. As a teacher, I realize that it's not simple to leave the classroom to walk with one student; however, it's possible that we can create a structure that allows for this. It may be possible for support personnel to cover a classroom for a few minutes. Or if they have a relationship with the child, they may be the one to step in. Likewise, in our school I've observed teachers stepping up to lend a hand even without a formal process in place. I recall a time when my teammate, Jamie Dauphinet, stepped up to walk and talk with a young child who was having a tough moment. The child's teacher required a break, and Dauphinet, who just happened to be passing by during her prep time, recognized the need to relieve the teacher. As educators dedicated to our learners, it's just what we do. We're there for all students in the school, not just our own.

As you connect with students, I challenge you to think of how you can innovate inside the box. If needed, could you take ten minutes of your lunch on occasion for a child who is struggling or even connect during flex time or study halls? Creatively restructure times during your day, or identify how you and colleagues can collaborate to provide more time to support learners. Creating cultures that provide emotional support encourages students to better engage in learning and formulate questions around their curiosities. In contrast, within a culture where threats and fear reign, learners are likely to either act out with behavior or clam up to avoid possible ridicule. Our schools are communities, and each classroom is a microcommunity of its own. By taking time to listen, validate, and connect with the heart, we foster the necessary environments that promote learning that leads to risk-taking.

Connect with Colleagues

So far, this chapter has focused on the need to connect and relate to students. Before we move on, I want to discuss another kind of relationship that has a tremendous impact on school culture: the relationships you have with your colleagues. You probably have some colleagues who are friends, some you seldom see, and others with whom you may frequently cross paths but rarely interact. You won't have the same depth of relationship with everyone in your school, but the more people with whom you can authentically connect in your school, the better chance you have at effecting positive change. The reason is simple: people are more likely to embrace shifts when a feeling of teamwork and positive relationship exists. When you know and understand your colleagues—and they you—you will be less likely to make negative assumptions and more likely to see connections regarding people's behaviors and their stories. As a bonus, experience has taught me that fostering genuine relationships with colleagues can lead to deep friendships.

The most impactful change occurs when we take the L.E.A.P. together, even if we're advancing at varying paces. To connect with colleagues, you can use the same three strategies you employ with students: be vulnerable and relatable, connect through experiences and listen, and validate your colleagues. It really can be that simple. A fellow educator shared with me that she overcame feeling isolated as an innovator by intentionally connecting and starting conversations with colleagues in her school. She took advantage of opportunities to smile, say hello, and ask about coworkers' families. She candidly shared successes and failures, was open about how she retooled or recovered from things that didn't go as planned, and welcomed advice from colleagues during staff meetings. She listened as her colleagues talked about struggles they were facing, she validated their feelings, and worked collaboratively to develop solutions. Over time, relationships blossomed, and her colleagues warmed to the ideas she had for their school. They even sought her input and partnered with her on projects to create meaningful learning experiences.

L.E.A.P. Onward

Innovation thrives where a culture of positive relationships, trust, and mutual respect exist because it is in these kinds of schools where students and teachers feel free to take risks within learning. Potential for change exists when just *one* individual begins forming connections with others to create widespread influence to improve and innovate. Take on the challenge of pulling others in. Create a hub of relationships where support and encouragement are the mainstays of your school's culture.

L.E.A.P. Tips and Takeaways

* Provide space for students to decompress.
* Remain patient and consistent. Walk away when necessary.
* Empower choice.
* Expose your vulnerabilities to be relatable.
* Celebrate effort and perseverance as often as you celebrate successes.
* Allow students to be codesigners of routines and protocols.

* Identify a reasonable solution that is fair to the learner and their unique situation.
* Greet your students daily and create an inviting environment.

L.E.A.P. beyond Your Boundaries

Share your reflections, questions, and ideas using #LEAPeffect.

1. How do you currently seek to develop relationships with learners and colleagues?
2. What are your next steps in moving forward to foster deeper connections with individuals?

Part II
Empowered Learning

Chapter 4
Fostering a Culture of Risk-Taking

The way to develop self-confidence is to do the thing you fear and get a record of successful experiences behind you. Destiny is not a matter of chance, it is a matter of choice; it is not a thing to be waited for, it is a thing to be achieved.

—William Jennings Bryan

In 1926, Albert May, my loving and devoted grandfather, whom we called Opa, courageously traveled to the United States from Bremerhaven, Germany. He was a mere eighteen years of age when he made the uncertain journey. The economy after WWI in Germany was vulnerable, and he looked forward to the opportunities in America despite vast uncertainties. Opa crossed the tumultuous Atlantic Ocean. He lived with his cousins on Long Island and sought new job opportunities. While Opa lacked formal education, he was a self-initiated learner. He quickly learned English as well as the skills of masonry, carpentry, and building. His dedication to growing himself and pursuing his passions was the start to a new life for Opa—and our family.

Opa's decision to embark on a courageous journey across the ocean isn't all that dissimilar to the journey educators embark on when making shifts toward innovation. George Couros also reflects on his father's journey from Greece to Canada in *The Innovator's Mindset,* noting that, "We often forget the changes our families went through to give us the opportunities we have today—to leave the world a better place. In the same way, our job as educators is to provide new and better opportunities for our students."[1] Couros also reminds us that "Change is the opportunity to do something amazing!"

Reimagining how we envision school and taking strides to empower learning may feel like a substantial venture. It is a leap *filled* with promise—and it is one that many educators avoid for fear of the unknown. Succeeding in this journey requires a growth mindset and perseverance, traits Opa exemplified. My mother, Karen May-Snyder, reflects, "My father had a strong inner resilience and accepted adversity as part of life. When an obstacle presented itself, he worked through it or around it." Isn't this the kind of tenacity we want our learners to develop?

Opa embodied the characteristics of a risk-taker as he embraced the joys and hardships that come with life. Time and again, he showed resiliency—the very thing our students need if they are going to thrive in a culture where risk-taking and, by extension, failure are part of everyday learning.

As we seek to foster this culture of risk-taking, we have to remember that every person and situation is unique. Levels of risk are grounded in perception. How far we step outside of our comfort zones is less important than the act of continually taking steps to grow beyond our boundaries. With that in mind, let's explore how we can empower our learners to move forward at their pace.

Risk to L.E.A.P.

"A whole new economy based upon creativity and innovation is emerging," notes John M. Eger, director of the Creative Economy Initiative at San Diego State University in an article for *Empowered Learner*. "We urgently need to redesign our K–12 to focus on preparing students for this new competition if we are going to survive, let alone succeed, in this new global economy."[2]

As educators, we feel the pressure to prepare learners for their unknown future, but we don't always know how to go about making necessary adjustments. I think this is particularly true in schools where educators are weighed down by cookie-cutter curriculums, mandated programs, and standardized assessments. If that happens to be your situation, you may feel as if you're wobbling on a tightrope attempting to balance mandates while simultaneously striving to craft authentic learning experiences for your learners. Innovative teaching, in situations like this, can feel risky and isolating. Even so, I encourage you to take that risk and find ways to meet mandates *while* making students' learning experiences meaningful. Even better, tap into those relationships with the colleagues I mentioned in the previous chapter to create a culture where you're taking steps forward *with* others. Remember: Everyone benefits when collective efforts foster a culture of risk-taking. Our students need for us to take that L.E.A.P. and provide the kind of flexible learning that will best prepare them for their future.

Creating a Culture of Risk-Taking in School

The following eight tenets will support you as you seek to create a culture where all learners—educators and students alike—are empowered to become responsible risk-takers who push boundaries and innovate.

Tenets to Create a Culture of Risk-Taking

* Cultivate relationships.
* Empower individuals.
* Celebrate together.
* Create a collaborate vision.
* Infuse passions and strengths.
* Communicate clearly.
* Have a culture of yes.
* Reflect and retool.

1. Cultivate relationships.

Relationships are essential for creating a culture of risk-taking. Trust empowers people to step out of their comfort zones, while positive interactions illuminate possibilities and individual potential.

2. Empower individuals.

Jimmy Casas writes in his book *Culturize,* "No one person was ever meant to lead a classroom, school, or district all alone, not if they want to propel the work that needs to be done to a maximum level of efficiency and to sustain a high quality of work over a long period of time."[3] If we are going to create sustainable shifts, we have to empower people—students and staff alike.

We empower individuals through demonstrating trust, delegating leadership roles, and building capacity in others. Empowered individuals don't feel the need to seek permission to take risks. They know that they're trusted and are confident that they have authority to make decisions that lead to the betterment of the shared vision. They don't wait for direction; they take action.

Importantly, let's note that it's not solely the responsibility of administrators to empower individuals. The synergy created when teachers empower one another can lead to incredible ideas being shared and implemented. Recognizing the work of others and encouraging them to share with colleagues are simple ways to empower other educators.

By the same token, students benefit from being empowered to take ownership of their learning and become leaders at school. When we empower learners, they develop the ability to think independently. Rather than awaiting directions from the teacher or doing what they believe would please their teacher, they can learn to set individual, class, and even school goals then create plans to achieve them. With routines and systems in place, even our youngest learners are capable of leading; they deserve to be empowered and supported as drivers of their learning.

3. Celebrate together.

Celebrating is a sure way to create a culture of risk-taking. Remember, what matters isn't how far you step on a single occasion, but that you are continually moving forward. The objective is to embody the innovator's mindset, craft authentic learning experiences for kids, continuously retool to improve, and remain committed as learners ourselves. When any one of those things happens in our schools, we need to celebrate!

Principal Bill Powers, EdD, shines a spotlight on staff by celebrating the efforts of his teachers. In our conversation, Powers shared, "Every time we get together as a staff, we celebrate. We open staff meetings with personal and professional celebrations. It's a great way to learn about one another."

Furthermore, Powers explained that each month, a different teacher is highlighted as the Teacher of the Month. Rather than this being a competition, it's a recognition each teacher will receive over time. After a teacher is selected, staff members are asked to share why the individual is an asset to their school. Powers then gathers responses from colleagues, he has them printed and placed in a frame that is presented to the chosen teacher during a staff meeting. What I appreciate about this exercise is that staff members are encouraged to think about *why* each of their colleagues is an asset. In return, the teacher gets to understand exactly how their colleagues view them. Any school could implement this practice to shine the light of celebration on its staff members and teachers. Every individual has potential to contribute to the school culture, and celebrating is a simple way to recognize each person's contributions.

Similarly, author of *The Pepper Effect,* principal, and founder of #CelebrateMonday, Sean Gaillard, enacts the "Be the Change Positive Principal Call" for teachers to uplift and celebrate staff. Gaillard looks for individuals who are attempting to be a positive change in what they're doing for kids or their colleagues and surprises them in class by celebrating their effort. He shared with me that when he makes the announcement, kids are just as thrilled as the teachers. Selected individuals receive a certificate and phone call to their family, and their picture is then shared on social media. Gaillard's commendable endeavor to celebrate individuals elevates culture and relationships.

Both tactics shared by Powers and Gaillard can be employed in the classroom, too! In our class, learners have contributed positive adjectives to describe their friends in word cloud creations. I frame the word clouds for each child to take home as a visual reminder of their strengths and of why they are important. It's an excellent way for students to recognize and honor the originality of their peers. Another way we celebrate individuals at our school is by making positive calls home. Inspired by Principal Mark French, who launched #GoodNewsCallOfTheDay, we too celebrate learners who continually give their best effort and those who demonstrate that they are working toward goals. Our learners are present when our principal, Patrick Patterson, makes the call so that they can share the moment with their family members.

We can foster a culture of celebration by empowering learners to display work that they're proud of, collaboratively develop cheers or chants for celebratory moments, and even identify mistakes that lead to new understandings and learning. Celebration cultivates a culture where individuals feel appreciated for their efforts.

4. Collaborative vision.

A culture of collaboration fosters an environment where we openly share and are transparent about our successes and challenges as we move toward our collective vision. When we collaboratively focus on improving student learning connected to our vision, we open the gateway to share new ideas and create unique strategies or approaches to personalize learning. Believing that our colleagues and we can collaboratively impact student achievement encourages us to develop a shared sense of collective efficacy, promoting risk-taking.

According to one study, "Collective efficacy increases when educators believe that they are capable of supporting students to master complex content, fostering students' creativity, and inspiring students to believe they can be successful in school. When efficacy is high, educators show greater persistence and are more likely to take risks by attempting new methods of teaching."[4]

A collaborative vision heightens collective efficacy and has the potential to catapult our L.E.A.P. to support learners within a rapidly changing learning environment; in fact, Professor John Hattie, researcher in education and author of *Visible Learning*, ranked collective teacher efficacy as the number *one* factor influencing student achievement.[5]

In the classroom, learners benefit from being involved in the development of the shared vision too. Rather than passively attending school each day, students can drive their learning experiences by developing the vision or classroom mission statement. Their vision can extend to classroom design to reflect their needs, interests, and celebrations. Provide examples and allow your learners to brainstorm independently and collaboratively to encourage the development of ideas. Morning meetings provide an excellent opportunity to reinforce the shared vision, reflect on progress, or retool if necessary.

5. Infuse interests and strengths.

Drawing on the interests and strengths of individuals increases their willingness to embrace risk-taking as it fuels confidence and motivation. Some schools use Edcamp-style staff meetings and conference days to create the opportunity for educators to share their strengths and passions while also learning from others in the room. According to the Edcamp Foundation, "Edcamps encourage individuals to recognize that they have something to contribute even if they're engaged in a conversation around a new trend in education."[6]

In October 2017, I attended an Edcamp session with colleagues on "Cultivating the Maker Mindset." Before we could discuss how to cultivate the maker mindset, it was critical that we all had a general understanding of maker education. Several individuals in our session communicated that they didn't know what maker education was, but were curious to learn. Others expressed interest in wanting to learn how to create a maker culture to help colleagues understand the value of maker education. Participants contributed to defining maker education and identifying the why behind it. With a common understanding, our discussion gained momentum. Every individual who jumped into the conversation had something to offer. Even the individuals new to maker education contributed by sharing inquiry strategies, organizational methods, design-thinking framework, STEAM resources, and more. It was exhilarating to bounce ideas off of one another, ask questions, and provide/receive various tips. What unfolded was that individuals contributed information based on their interests and strengths that related to the concept of maker education.

Edcamps provide a flexible environment where educators have the option to take risks at their own pace. By supporting individuals to infuse their interests and strengths into their learning and teaching, we develop the capacity to transform our level of engagement and that of our students.

In the same way, when we provide time and space for *learners* to explore their strengths and interests (discussed further in Chapter 8), they discover and develop their passions. Crafting opportunities to infuse passion into education—both for educators and learners—creates meaningful learning experiences.

6. Unambiguous communication.

While some teachers are energized by pushing the envelope, others require support and reassurance to move forward. Regardless, all educators benefit from explicit support from administrators and colleagues. Unambiguous communication is critical in creating a culture of risk-taking. As humans, our brains are continuously processing and analyzing the behaviors of others, which leads to the development of perceived messages. We may say we support responsible risk-taking that leads to growth, but our body language, tone, or our word choice may send a conflicting message. Our job as educators is to communicate clearly so that our learners are empowered to stretch and grow.

Director of Secondary Education Neil Gupta, EdD, spoke with me about how his district fosters the conditions to promote a culture of risk-taking. Gupta shared that from the district-level perspective, their superintendent, Trent Bowers, EdD, sets the stage to support risk-taking by establishing and sharing expectations. When expectations regarding risk-taking are explicitly stated by administrators, educators become aware that support exists for them with certain parameters. Additionally, Bowers communicates his "Six Expectations" with the whole staff at his first district-wide convocation. "The expectations were to 1) Be Kind to Kids, 2) Be Present, 3) Serve the Customer, 4) Communicate, Communicate, Communicate, 5) Believe in Growth, *and* 6) Be Kind to Kids," explained Gupta.

In their district, Bowers encourages district and building leaders to share stories that highlight the fantastic work teachers are doing for the sake of kids. Bowers works with the district communications team to follow up with the individuals to curate stories and sometimes create videos to help share them on social media and the district's website. The communication continues through emails to staff and community, all of which reinforce the positive things happening in the schools. Highlighting stories of educators and what's happening in their classrooms validates the district's values as well as the work its teachers are doing.

By sharing the six expectations and capturing stories to promote them, Bowers actively shows his support for risk-taking through innovation to empower student learning. While innovation is heavily steeped in risk-taking, communicating the expectations provides a framework for success. By empowering staff members to make decisions with a roadmap based on what's best for kids, staff members feel confident that taking responsible risks will be appreciated and supported by their administration. And as administrators join the trek toward innovation alongside teachers, by experimenting with new methods, they further demonstrate their unwavering support.

Learners also need to feel safe to take risks. You can foster growth in students by clearly communicating (in word and action) that you value their questions and ideas and want to hear their thoughts. Smile, look your kids in the eyes, and take the time to listen. Communicate what you value through celebrating efforts and engaging in individual conversations. As educators, we communicate that we care by being responsive to the needs of our learners and modeling open-mindedness in classroom discussions. Harnessing the power of effective communication fosters a culture of risk-taking.

7. Culture of yes.

In a conversation with fellow educators in a Facebook group, a team of teachers told me about a book study they had done that focused on inspiring creativity within students through writing. Filled with excitement related to the possibilities, they were prepared to innovate within the writing process. Several weeks later, I checked back in with them to hear about their progress, and their excitement had skyrocketed! Hesitant to bring this idea to their new administrator due to past experiences of hearing no from their previous principal, they were uncertain if they'd be able to use their new process to replace the district-mandated writing prompts that lacked creativity and originality. Determined that it was worth the risk, these teachers shared their process with the principal and explained their why, along with the supporting evidence and resources that indicated their goals and how they would go about achieving them. Their principal not only said yes in support of their ideas, he also offered to help ensure their success. Although they couldn't eliminate the district-mandated writing prompts, they worked together to identify ways to innovate within the writing process. With their principal's support, the teachers felt confident to step forward as innovators. They recognized that shifts can sometimes feel challenging and may be messy, but by collaboratively reflecting and retooling to refine their efforts, they could empower their students to succeed as writers. Kudos to those teachers for taking a risk *and* to the principal for supporting their work—and collaborating with them!

If we take steps to develop a shared vision around our why, analyze how to meet the needs of our learners best, and take into account how we can empower learning, we ought to be able to take the L.E.A.P. with encouragement from others. Finding opportunities to say yes in the classroom has the potential to revolutionize your culture. Establishing a culture of yes may require us to relinquish control. But, in doing so, we can catalyze risk-taking in schools and classrooms. Learners empowered as leaders in a culture of yes develop the necessary skill sets to contribute to new structures and routines. Sure, it can feel foreign to say yes if we're accustomed to developing all of the expectations and giving directions throughout the day.

Consider some of the areas in which you call all of the shots, then select one area you feel comfortable loosening your grip and begin there. In my own classroom, I started with the first twenty-five minutes of our day. It is standard practice for teachers to give an assignment as "busy work" to occupy learners as they arrive to the classroom. To foster a culture of yes, I communicated to my learners that, since our vision includes developing a joy to come to school and engage in exploration to inspire learning, we were going to reimagine our mornings. Together we brainstormed all of the possibilities and co-created the concept of maker mornings. Learners were empowered to choose how they started each day and what they wanted to explore based on their passions and curiosity. This is just one example of how to spark a culture of yes, and I assure you that we can identify many ways to incorporate yes to foster a culture where learners feel free to make unsolicited responses rather than feel confined by constant constraints.

8. Reflection and retooling.

Deep reflection is necessary for supporting us to create a culture of risk-taking. Reflection is the vehicle that drives us to think critically about our effort, attitudes, and growth toward taking the L.E.A.P. When educators engage in deep and purposeful reflective conversations, we learn from one another and have the opportunity to support each other in the retooling process. Knowing that we will reconvene to reflect and retool encourages us to grow as risk-takers because it eliminates the feeling that there's a finality to our work. If we make a mistake or feel that we failed in our endeavor, there's no need to revert to traditional ways. Instead, we can reflect on the occurrences and retool by shifting strategies or resources.

Throughout the first year my team and I launched project-based learning, we engaged in reflective conversations daily. We faced moments where we felt uncertain about the direction we were going with our students (despite in-depth planning with the support of Buck Institute for Education), but we grew stronger as we reflected on what we observed in the classroom and retooled.

Our learners benefit from being engaged in frequent deep reflection too. This includes quiet individual reflection as well as reflective conversations with others. Reflection is one of the most important aspects of learning—and something we need to carve time out for students and ourselves to engage in.

> ## We do not learn from experience; we learn from reflecting on experience.
> ### —John Dewey

Embody the Tenets of a Risk-Taker

My grandfather, Opa, embodied the tenets of a risk-taker. Even though his family in Germany was deeply saddened by his choice to create a new life in the United States, they supported his decision because they respected his aspirations. Having identified his passions, strengths, and a vision for the life he desired, he seized opportunities to learn new skills. With each job he took, he adapted to varying expectations through the process of reflection. Retooling his craft allowed him to develop stronger skills, which, in turn, provided him with improved opportunities for work. After a brutal battle against cancer, Opa passed when I was thirteen years old. I was in awe of the number of individuals from our community who came to pay their respects. Time and again, individuals spoke of Opa's selfless nature and how he always put the needs of others before his own. Relationships were of utmost importance to Opa. In my own life, I carry his legacy with me as a reminder that life is about connecting with people in meaningful ways and taking risks to reach our greatest potential.

L.E.A.P. Onward

Taking risks may feel daunting, but employing any one of the eight tenets can encourage us to begin taking the L.E.A.P. Seeing improvement in learning due to our collective efforts is incredibly gratifying. With each step, growth occurs that continues to propel us forward. A culture where individuals feel supported to take risks serves as the catalyst for learning transformation.

L.E.A.P. Tips and Takeaways:

* Don't just say you support individuals; model it through your actions.
* Be conscious of how words, tones, and actions promote or hinder your message of risk-taking.
* Empower individuals to take risks by demonstrating trust and autonomy.
* Celebrate accomplishments of others and create spaces where individuals can celebrate themselves or each other.
* Engage in frequent collaboration to drive toward the shared vision, and develop a sense of collective efficacy.
* Infuse passions and strengths to inspire individuals to contribute at the highest level.
* Dare to relinquish control and say yes to new ideas and possibilities.

L.E.A.P. beyond Your Boundaries

Share your reflections, questions, and ideas using #LEAPeffect.

1. How do you currently support and encourage risk-taking in your school or classroom?
2. Which of these tenets do you feel would be the most powerful in fostering a culture of risk-taking in your school or classroom based on where you currently are in your journey?
3. How will you approach infusing this tenet regularly into your routines?

Chapter 5
Reimagining Learning

Whatever you can do or dream you can, begin it.
Boldness has genius, power, and magic in it.

—Goethe

Imagine this: You're at home eagerly awaiting your college acceptance letter. Rather than the classic large rectangular envelope arriving in the mail, you notice a curious-looking silver, cylindrical tube. You pop open the container, and in it is your acceptance letter to the college of your choice, The Massachusetts Institute of Technology! Excitement surges throughout your body, and your heart pounds faster, as this was the moment you'd been waiting for! As you read the letter more closely, you see a message that intrigues you and provokes your imagination. It's an invitation to come up with a clever hack using the tube in which the acceptance letter arrived. It closes with a reminder that "the possibilities are as infinite as your MIT imagination."[1]

Erin King, class of 2016, received her acceptance letter to MIT at age seventeen. With the spirit of a true hacker, she went all out, using the tube to create what she called a "Tubecam." She launched the

Tubecam, equipped with a GPS-enabled GoPro Hero and carrying her acceptance letter, approximately 17.2 miles in the sky. She recovered the Tubecam from a small patch of trees and posted the video of its journey into near space. In the time-lapse YouTube video that

curates the experience, King can be seen designing her Tubecam alongside her father. You can check out her radical hack on YouTube.[2]

Empowered to use her imagination, she exhibited traits of creative thinking, which led to an innovative concept. King took initiative, set a goal, harnessed technology as a tool, effectively communicated in collaboration with others,

Erin King's MIT Hack

figured out what materials she required as well as the wind patterns for her idea to take flight (literally). In her video documentation, you can see how diligently she worked and the excitement of everyone involved. Talk about learning in action!

I love that spirit of ingenuity and hacking, and *I* want to be like King and play around with ideas for reimagining learning by hacking what we currently do. I also want our schools to support the development of these traits in our learners. I'm going to go out on a limb and say that most schools are not challenging learners to think or dream or hack at the kind of level that is required for success in our rapidly changing world. Yes, it happens in pockets in some of our schools, or periodically throughout the year. And, of course, there are schools that place a unique emphasis on developing these skills and harnessing the strengths of learners. I see and hear about educators who are reimagining learning and supporting learners to develop agency. So many are hacking traditional education and seeing excellent results! In King's case, it's probable that she benefited from educators who promoted divergent thinking and empowered learning. Our goal must be to ensure that we provide learning opportunities that foster creative thinking and personal initiative throughout all schools.

The challenge we need to overcome is that our schools were designed during the Industrial Revolution with the goal of developing compliant and productive workers who would eventually serve in factories. Schools were not founded on the premise of igniting a culture of innovation. They were designed to meet the primary need during that era, which was to crank out workers who could help make factories run as efficiently as possible. People were trained to do as they were told to work *for someone else.*

Life has changed, and so must education. As Founder and CEO of StartEdUp, Don Wettrick, notes, "According to several research studies, between 45–50 percent of our nation's jobs will be freelance or gig economies. And what is education doing? Doubling down on compliance."[3] Today, we desperately need individuals who are adaptable to the changing times. It's time to take the L.E.A.P. and reimagine learning with the understanding that it will continue to evolve as our world changes at a rapid pace.

Just "Google It"

The day before a social studies test, my son asked me, "Why do I need to memorize information for a test? If I'm outside the classroom, I can just Google the answer. Is it just to test how well I can memorize facts?" Julian is incredibly witty and, at thirteen, looks to challenge conventional thinking. He makes a valid point. In many schools, students are expected to passively consume content and regurgitate it on an assessment. Assessments serve the necessary goal of gaining feedback on our learners' understanding. We can use it as a guide to personalize subsequent learning. I'm not saying all tests are bad.

What I am saying is that it may no longer be necessary for kids to simply memorize information for the sake of memorization. Our goal should now be developing learners who know where to locate information, how to discern the credibility of resources, and how to apply the information to learning projects in a purposeful and meaningful manner. Learners also benefit from gaining experience as problem *finders*. Problem finding compels creativity, and innovative thinking emerges. Identifying and understanding the problems that exist drives us to contemplate and construct unique solutions.

While the focus of society has shifted from a need for compliance and memorization to initiative and creative thinking, some learners still yearn for their teachers to simply tell them what to do so that they can readily complete their task. (And some teachers are happy to oblige them.) But if we are going to prepare students for the world we live in, we must foster learner agency.

Foster Learner Agency

Katie Martin, PhD, author of *Learner-Centered Innovation*, writes, "Learner agency is about moving students from passively responding to acting with purpose to reach a desired goal or outcome."[4] This is exactly what high school teacher Dave Black strives to do. Black has reimagined education through crafting project-based learning (PBL) opportunities that support students to pursue passions and develop ownership for their learning. PBL incorporates inquiry-based learning, which can be messy compared to traditional teaching. The results are worth it, however, when learners develop intrinsic motivation because they're empowered to identify questions or problems associated with their interests.

Drafting driving questions is an element of PBL, which means Black intentionally engages learners in the practice of crafting quality questions. He recognizes that kids are accustomed to being asked questions that have either a right or wrong answer connected to them. While Black has seen growth in his learners, he admits that struggles still exist. "By the time students reach their junior year, passive learning has become ingrained, as they've experienced it (passive learning) since third or fourth grade. It becomes a habit that has become comfortable and just the way it is. Kids are resigned to how school is and are trying to get by the best they can," he notes. As educators, our job is to break down that attitude of passiveness in our students.

Seeing passive learning take place is one of many reasons I'm deeply passionate about reimagining learning and developing a community where we can support one another to take the L.E.A.P. In his quest to foster learner agency, Black assures his kids, "This is going to feel uncomfortable, but you *will* get it." He challenges them to think differently about the world around them. Black approaches this activity by infusing his own passions in learning. Because he is passionate about baseball, he took his class to Coors Field in Denver, Colorado, for a field trip. His goal was not to push his passion on learners, but to immerse them in the opportunity to craft quality questions through observation while getting a 360-degree view of the world in a way that captivates them and sparks curiosity. If Black would have just talked about or had learners ask questions pertaining to baseball, only a handful of students would've had the background experience of attending or watching a game. When we provide experiences for learners that allow them to observe and take notice of what captures their attention, we ensure that all students are on a level playing field.

As his learners observed their surroundings at the stadium, they brainstormed as many questions as possible. Questions may come slowly at first if it is a new concept or practice. But as learners persist through the activity, wonderings develop and questions begin to flow—particularly when individuals brainstorm with others. Often, one question will spawn another. Black's students generated six pages of questions from that one experience! Listed below is a small example—from the day Black's learners spent time observing their surroundings at Coors Field—demonstrating how one question leads to another. After drafting their questions, learners then selected the one that most rouses immense curiosity in them, and developed it as the driving question within PBL.

* What is the job description for the main writers from newspapers for the team?
* How did these writers get their jobs in following the teams?
* What must one do to be accredited for a game as a member of the press?
* How has social media changed writing and reports?
* Who are the people that create blogs about the team?
* What is the relationship between bloggers and traditional print and broadcast media?

Taking kids outside the classroom walls has the potential to invoke zeal and awaken senses. If you are unable to take your class on a field trip, provide the opportunity for learners to get outside on school grounds to engage in an activity similar to this. Many schools leverage Google Cardboard for virtual field trips, and you and I both know that products such as Google Cardboard will continue to evolve and be developed with the progression of technology. When learners draft questions and allow their thoughts to evolve, curiosity is often provoked. I believe this is a practice that teachers of all grade levels could employ to stimulate divergent thinking and experience wonder, leading to awe.

Shifting from Teacher Driven
to Learner Centered

**It is literally neurobiologically
impossible to think deeply about
things you don't care about.
—MH Immordino-Yang**

Reimagining learning requires us to shift the paradigm from preparing learners for the industrial age to designers and cocreators of learning who assimilate how to navigate and adapt in a complex global society. Education Reimagined articulates,

The learner-centered paradigm changes our very view of learners themselves. Learners are seen and known as wondrous, curious individuals with vast capabilities and limitless potential. This paradigm recognizes that learning is a lifelong pursuit and that our natural excitement and eagerness to discover and learn should be fostered through-out our lives, particularly in our earliest years. Thus, in this paradigm, learners are active participants in their learning as they gradually become owners of it, and learning itself is seen as an engaging and exciting process. Each child's interests, passions, dreams, skills, and needs shape his or her learning experience and drive the commitments and actions of the adults and communities supporting him or her.[5]

As a parent, I wonder how often my own sons' interests, strengths, and dreams are interwoven into their learning experience. I'm grateful for the educators who have bonded with my children by recognizing and honoring their strengths as they've encouraged their growth. But I know, too, that weaving students' strengths and passions into learning requires their teachers, and all of us, to think differently. Education Reimagined redefines what it means to be a learner today, and this has direct implications on our behaviors as educators. In taking the L.E.A.P., we need to explore how we can shift from teacher driven to student centered by reimagining learning and how we view learners.

Learners can become co-pioneers in their education and promote the development of empowerment in a student-centered learning environment, where adults shift from the role of teacher to coach. In this role, we can craft learning experiences that are unique to the students' passions, strengths, and needs. As with any shift, success comes when we take gradual steps forward—from one move to the next. I used to frequently refer to the 4Cs of learning, which traditionally include creativity, communication, collaboration, and critical thinking. George Couros challenged my thinking on the 4Cs by sharing an article with me titled "Curiosity is the Cat" by Will Richardson.

In the article, Richardson comments, "When it comes to learning, what comes before curiosity?" After reading the article, I realized that in my focus on the 4Cs, I had neglected to recognize a vital component that serves as the bedrock of reimagining learning: curiosity. After all, it's the pinnacle of what I believe drives us as beings, and I leverage it daily in learning. In response to the question he posed, Richardson states,

> Critical thinking doesn't, because if you're not curious
> as to whether something is true or fake or accurate or real,
> you won't really think very hard about it. Creativity doesn't,

because making stuff is borne out of the curiosity of "What if?" What if I try this note here? What if I apply this touch of paint there? What if I mixed these two things together, or built another arm on that robot, or . . . Communication doesn't come before curiosity, because if you're not curious about your audience, if you're not using curiosity-driven empathy to craft your message, it probably won't get across. And collaboration? Isn't that rooted in the curiosity of what other people might know and contribute to your own learning? People don't collaborate for the sake of collaborating . . . except in schools, of course.[6]

I concur with Richardson. No matter how you look at it, curiosity is crucial to inspire learning. We as educators need to rekindle our own curiosity while igniting the curiosity within our learners to foster an unquenchable thirst for exploration. That curiosity will lead to authentic learning discoveries. When planning instruction, we must place an intentional emphasis on how we will invoke curiosity as a means to captivate learners. Reimagining learning requires us to look through the lens of our students.

6Cs of Reimagining Learning

In my quest to reimagine learning, I reflected on what has bolstered learner agency and fostered a student-centered learning environment in my classroom and in classrooms around the world. The following 6Cs serve as catalysts that inspire learners to reveal their capabilities and potential. While components of the 6Cs exist in classrooms in pockets, more often than not, they happen sporadically throughout the school week. Unfortunately, entire classrooms of learners are starving for the 6Cs. As we reimagine education, these

6Cs are essential to maintain a healthy culture of learning. Included are curiosity, creativity, communication, critical thinking, collaboration, and connectedness. While this chapter serves as an entry point for each of the 6Cs, we'll continue exploring them throughout both Parts II and III as they're embedded in stories and examples.

As you explore the 6Cs, allow your curiosity to wonder how you might infuse them into your instructional approaches.

Curiosity

Curiosity inspires learners to ask, "Why does this occur?" or "How does this make sense?" or "I wonder...?" Curiosity has the potential to ignite creativity, wonder, and awe. It engages us to think critically about problems and inspires us to open up as communicators in collaboration with others. Learners are more likely to deeply engage in critical thinking and flourish in creativity with curiosity. It drives learners to be passionate about *wanting* to learn rather than *having* to learn.

L.E.A.P. Tips to Foster Curiosity

* Carve out time to wonder and generate questions that spark curiosity.
* Pose unique open-ended problems or scenarios and allow learners to contemplate all the possibilities.
* Provide learners with materials or resources that foster exploration and allow them to learn through trial and error, engaging as a guide on the side.
* Incorporate passions and making into learning, in addition to choice, to explore independent curiosities.
* Scaffold learning to support those beginning to identifying problems to further develop as problem finders.

Creativity

Creativity is not limited to the arts. Creativity can occur in all areas of learning and fosters divergent thinking. Just think of how creativity boosted the success of Google, Apple, Snapchat, Uber, Airbnb, and Amazon. Purposeful creativity is powerful as it leads to innovative ideas and new possibilities. In our learning, we incorporate creativity in all areas. This even includes mathematics, as learners are immersed in opportunities to problem-solve creatively, design their own problems, and are encouraged to integrate art as well as the world around them. Empowering learners to demonstrate their understanding creatively through the use of technology, making, or designing captivates their focus and drives learning.

L.E.A.P. Tips to Foster Creativity

* Facilitate learning through employing the process of design thinking (more in Chapter 9).
* Leverage technology as a creative tool to demonstrate and share ideas or create new concepts.
* Provide opportunities for learners to ponder new ideas or ways of looking at what currently exists.
* Create opportunities to engage in passion-based learning to connect with content in a personal way, along with time to use meaningful materials to make, enhancing connections for retention.
* Empower learners with choice in how to express ideas and learning.
* Learn based on problems to be solved with alternative avenues of thinking.

Communication

Communication can foster synergistic energy amongst learners if properly leveraged. Be intentional about creating a culture where learners understand the art of conversation. The strategy of think-pair-share, taking time to contemplate a question or problem, then discussing it with a partner, can be effective only if learners are actively engaged in understanding the purpose behind conversations. When learners understand the benefits, that participating in discussion with a partner assists the brain in processing information to make meaning of it, they are more likely to develop ownership over the way they attend to the conversation. We also want to support learners to develop as active listeners who respond appropriately. Accountable talk or collaborative conversation sentence stems support even the youngest learners by engaging in authentic conversations that may challenge or affirm thinking or spark new ideas.

L.E.A.P. Tips to Foster Communication

* Be intentional about practicing the art of conversations.
* Model high-quality statements and thoughtful responses.
* Provide anchor charts or other resources that have sentence stems visible to support learners in sharing their thoughts and responding to the thoughts of others.
* Expose learners to deep questions or compelling concepts that provoke curiosity or require learners to form opinions.
* Facilitate Socratic seminars where learners in the inner circle take turns engaging in evidence-based discussions while others in the outer circle observe, take notes, and provide feedback.
* Utilize web-based platforms, such as Google Classroom and Seesaw, where learners can communicate beyond the

walls of the classroom while also supporting learners to be positive digital citizens.

Critical Thinking

With the complexity of our world and the vast amount of information that's available, our learners benefit from developing critical thinking skills. Critical thinking fosters learners to improve their ability to reason, make decisions, and make judgments to effectively problem-solve. With all of the advancements in our world, we still have fundamental issues that are left unsolved, including topics such as climate change, clean energy, and suitable drinking water that's accessible for all. We want our learners to be problem finders who think critically about how to address them. Critical thinking leads to better judgment, evaluation, and encourages us to listen with empathy to understand alternate viewpoints.

L.E.A.P. Tips to Foster Critical Thinking

* Immerse students in inquiry-based learning where they can grapple with perplexing questions.
* Expose learners to authentic problems within the school, your community, and our world for contemplation. Have them engage in effective conversations with peers to challenge thinking.
* Empower learners to grapple with reliability of information and its usefulness to their project or work.
* Encourage learners to look at problems differently. Ask: Is there more than one way to solve the problem? How many ways could you solve the problem? What if _____ changed?
* Provide constraints in the design process that encourage alternative measures.

Collaboration

Learners of all ages require a balance between independent thinking and reflection time alongside opportunities to collaborate. Meaningful collaboration combines the strength, talents, and passions of individuals to create a stronger product or result than if completed independently. I strategically structure collaboration in several ways depending on what learners are exploring; for example, there are some situations where learners benefit from brainstorming individually and then sharing ideas with their team. Other times, learners will brainstorm together first, retool the concept independently, and then return to share their thinking. Teams then either write or draw and label their ideas/thoughts on iPads, paper, or dry erase boards. Following that, we engage in gallery walks with our team members to observe, honor, and discuss the thinking of other teams. At the conclusion, we come together to share what we notice, wonder, and how it influences our original thinking. Collaboration is impactful when learners have developed the foundational skill set of effective communication by pushing one another to think critically, and has the potential to increase creative measures leading to heightened curiosity.

L.E.A.P. Tips to Foster Collaboration

* Focus heavily on the development of effective communication skills.
* Provide time for independent thinking to support learners to identify their original thoughts and ideas prior to coming together to discuss.
* Promote open-mindedness by fostering the understanding that there is often more than one solution to a problem.
* Develop a culture where individuals honor their unique strengths and talents as well as those of their peers.

* Employ protocols that streamline collaboration and provide structure and make necessary adjustments to fit the needs of your learners.

Connectedness

In reimagining learning, developing connectedness elevates experiences and expands global perspectives. Isolation is no longer necessary as technology advances and provides us with opportunities to connect beyond our walls. Today, learners and educators can connect with individuals who can collaborate or contribute to learning experiences in our schools locally and globally. Our class has partnered with two classes, with teachers Rachel Lamb and Steven Thomas from New Mexico, to collaborate on a STEAM challenge where learners develop an airbag system to protect an egg when dropped. The goal was to create a model based on the premise of how NASA successfully dropped rovers onto the surface of Mars. Connecting our classes opened the world to all of our learners as they processed the concept of a time difference, temperature of northeast versus southwest, variations in names as well as favorite foods. Our classes have shared learning via social media, posted designs on PBS Kids (Design Squad Global), and blogged about their experiences. Sure, we could have completed the STEAM challenge in isolation, but the experience was more abundant due to connectedness.

L.E.A.P. Tips to Foster Connectedness

* Identify local and global problems and connect with experts who will enrich learning.
* Participate in Mystery Skype, Mystery Number, or similar concepts that require classes to connect virtually to communicate, collaborate, and problem-solve together in a way that sparks curiosity and creativity.

* Blog for an authentic audience to share questions, learning, reflections, and seek feedback, along with new ideas.
* Leverage technology to connect, collaborate, and communicate with learners and educators throughout ongoing projects.

L.E.A.P. Onward

Infusing the 6Cs has transformed my classroom. Today, it is an environment that supports student-centered learning. When students are copilots or drivers of their educational experiences, they develop a greater appreciation for learning as a result. I strive to reframe the thinking of students to chip away at the mold of compliant, passive learning and support kids to draw on their passions to design and implement authentic projects. Learners embrace the 6Cs as they identify problems they're curious about, leverage creativity as they develop authentic projects, engage in critical thinking, and collaborate with others who enrich their learning. Connectedness is demonstrated as they create blogs to reflect on their learning, contribute to our class YouTube channel, and post on social media with my support to share with the world. I believe that every one of us can infuse the 6Cs of reimagining learning. Let's foster them until they begin to occur naturally and contribute to a student-centered learning environment. Now is the time to take the L.E.A.P. and reimagine learning so that students feel empowered to accomplish authentic work and contribute to their educational journey.

L.E.A.P. beyond Your Boundaries

Share your reflections, questions, and ideas using #LEAPeffect.

1. In what ways do you currently integrate the 6Cs of reimagining learning in your classroom or school?
2. Which of the Cs do you focus on the most? The least?
3. With the goal being to foster a learning environment that is student centered, where the 6Cs occur more naturally, how will you infuse the 6Cs of reimagining learning to hack what you currently do in your classroom or school?

Chapter 6
Empowering Learners

> Our job is obvious; we need to get out of
> the way, shine a light, and empower a new
> generation to teach itself and to go further
> and faster than any generation ever has.
>
> —Seth Godin

As a child, I would frequently find on my dresser library books that had been checked out by my mother. My response to finding those books varied. As a young child and tween, I felt excited by the surprise of a new book to read. During my teen years, I'm pretty sure I may have rolled my eyes a few times. Regardless, she continued to share books my way with positive intent.

My mother was determined to raise me to be an independent and confident individual. She immersed me in literature that told stories of adventurous individuals who went against the odds to challenge expectations and traditional thinking. Around the age of ten or so, I recall reading the biography of Amelia Earhart. I related to her personality because, like me, she enjoyed taking remarkable risks.

Reading her story made me feel invincible. It also helped me believe that anything is possible if you work for it. Earhart grew up during a time when it was inconceivable for women to independently pilot a plane. In 1920, Amelia took her first airplane ride, and the experience sparked a passion within her. After that flight, Earhart said, "By the time I had got two or three hundred feet off the ground, I knew I had to fly." Although her father felt some trepidation about his daughter flying, it was her mother who encouraged Amelia's passions by using some of her inheritance to purchase her daughter's plane.[1] In a letter to her husband, Amelia wrote, "Please know I am quite aware of the hazards . . . . I want to do it because I want to do it. Women must try to do things as men have tried. When they fail, their failure must be but a challenge to others."[2]

Today, the challenge in education is for *all* of us to reach for new levels of learning—and persevere through failure. Earhart's mother empowered her to pursue her passion, and, in return, Earhart left a legacy that continues to inspire others take the L.E.A.P. in all they desire to do. In this chapter, we're going to explore how we can awaken our learners' passions and empower them to soar.

Compliance, Engagement, Empowerment—What's the Difference?

In talking with a fellow educator about the difference between engagement and empowerment in the classroom, he asked me, "How does engagement look different than empowerment in your class-room?" I explained that engagement occurs through incorporating novelty, curiosity, elements of game-based learning, conversations, etc. Every classroom should be engaging as we want learners to feel interested *and* excited about learning. If, however, learners are continually asking for permission to use an iPad as a tool to construct knowledge or to sit elsewhere in the classroom, for example, they are not empowered as leaders of their learning.

In my own classroom, learners often start the school year with a compliant mindset. They seek approval from me as the teacher and look for signals that help them determine how they should behave. This mindset became especially evident the year I launched flexible seating. I had to tackle the process of assisting students to unlearn the compliant behavior of sitting where they were instructed. Selecting seating without guidance appeared too open-ended for them at first. They benefited from structure that provided a process for choosing their seat for the next day, prior to leaving the day before. Within the flexible structure, they identified seating that worked best for them and began to decipher when to move throughout the day to meet their individualistic and teaming needs. Eventually, we arrived at the point where learners no longer relied on the structure for selecting their classroom location, and I have learned that some groups require more time and some less to adjust to flexible seating choices.

Engagement shifts to empowerment when learners take ownership over their learning versus being engaged during an activity assigned by the teacher. When students initiate their learning, select their seating to suit their needs, and feel comfortable choosing the best tools to construct knowledge, that's when you know they feel *empowered*. Empowerment is a game-changer, particularly when you intentionally infuse learners' interests.

This graphic serves as a great visual representation that demonstrates student agency as a continuum.

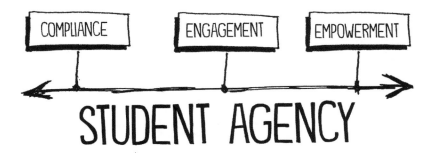

The journey toward student empowerment can feel intimidating to some. Outstanding classroom management is billed as an indicator of a successful educator, so we may fear that anything less than complete control makes us appear inept. What do you think when you hear the words student-led classrooms?

If you're like some educators, a chaotic, out-of-control classroom may be the first mental image you get. Don't worry, I'm not proposing that you allow chaos to reign. Some form of management is necessary, particularly when you're working with younger children. It's in these younger classrooms that "management through bribes" using public charts or the like tend to be the go-to move. But I'd like to propose an alternative approach through which you can support learners to take the initiative as active members of the classroom community through relationships, engagement, and empowerment. Yes, learners benefit from feedback based on their effort, but it is important to consider the method we use to provide that feedback and the implications that may accompany it. When we publicly display how a child is doing behaviorally, it can be perceived as a form of shaming, rather than encouraging a child to do better. The inadvertent message these public reports send is that children who are on red, rather than green, or have three strikes, are "bad." For this reason, among others, behavior charts are ineffective at shifting behavior. Sure, you may see short-term gains, but in the long run, they do more harm than good.[3] Children need to grasp how to regulate through identifying their needs and knowing how to meet them.

We can work alongside learners, giving positive verbal feedback on how their choices are appreciated and affect the culture of learning. We can create outlets to decompress, provide sensory-related activities for learners to engage in, offer choice in learning, and allow children to take movement breaks when they need to.

The ultimate goal of empowering students is to shift the culture so that they become invested in their learning and therefore are deeply engaged—not learning out of compliance, but out of excitement.

If, in your experience, learners are reliant on charts or systems, it may be helpful to begin with a private system (something not displayed publicly on the classroom wall) and focus on identifying positive effort. As you incorporate learning experiences that are relevant, deeply engaging, and empowering within an environment of authentic relationships, you can shift away from using a system as the culture of learning develops.

Additional Reasons to Shift Toward Empowered Learning

In a conversation with David Conley, PhD—founder of EdImagine and professor of educational policy and leadership at the University of Oregon's College of Education—that focused on empowering learning, he shared with me the nine skills all learners need to succeed:

1. Initiative
2. Independence
3. Personal management
4. High aspirations and goal orientation
5. Challenging conventions and assumptions

6. Persistence
7. Utilizing technology as a learning tool
8. Help-seeking
9. Ability to persist through failure

Empowerment supports the critical development of each of these skills. We must make our schools places where learners explore, inquire, create, and connect beyond the walls to share and learn with others. When I asked Conley about his view on empowerment, he replied that we need to know our learners today and meet them where they are right now:

> One thing about empowerment and self-knowledge is that students can learn on their own and are often learning outside of school to a much greater degree. I don't think educators have processed this. Educators are still operating under the assumption that the only things that are important to learn are what's taught in school—and the only way to learn it is to have a teacher tell you about it and test you on it. School doesn't prepare learners for how the workforce operates. You've got this disconnect because schools are often cut off from the outside world.

Pittsfield Middle-High School in New Hampshire is one place that *isn't* disconnected from the outside world and provides a prime example of how empowered learning can reshape the school experience for learners; in fact, the school shifted from being labeled a dropout factory to a *transformative student-centered learning environment* where learners thrive as a result of empowerment. English teacher at Pittsfield Middle-High School, Jennifer Wellington, shares that their school district has renovated its approach to learning through personalization and a lot of enthusiasm. Rather than being driven by grades, learners have several opportunities to demonstrate mastery. Once they realize that failure is not final, they begin to take risks, which actively engages them in their learning. In her own class, Wellington supports learners to develop their own questions and select the format for the class that works best for them. They're empowered to be the codesigners in learning. "Part of student-centered learning is asking the class what they need to make the class work," she says. "It has to be about going into the classroom and letting go of your ego, and teachers are not comfortable giving up power," Wellington explains. "But I don't see it as giving up power; I see it as shared power that makes the job a lot easier."[4]

Climbing the Ladder of Empowerment

You can make the journey toward empowering students easier for everyone involved by scaffolding a gradual shift of control. Shifting toward a student-centered learning environment where learner agency is fostered requires educators to approach teaching through the lens of a coach rather than a conductor. Moving from the teacher telling to having students take the lead is the biggest shift in climbing the ladder of empowerment. Empowering learners means that we are providing a vibrant environment that nourishes the development of critical skills our students require to be successful in today's world and their future.

While there are numerous ways in which we can support learners to develop the success skills needed to promote learner agency and empowerment, the following five approaches yield significant results:

1. Engaging in productive struggle
2. Leveraging technology as a tool
3. Choice-infused learning

4. Personal goal setting
5. Reflection

Engaging in Productive Struggle

Productive struggle fosters learners to develop grit and demonstrate creativity in problem solving as they contemplate how to grasp the problem at hand. Instinct and training may push us toward showing our learners the process of how to solve a problem before empowering them to engage in a productive struggle. Although our intentions are good, we may be depriving them of valuable learning. Which is why, rather than demonstrating the process of solving, I prefer to approach teaching through coaching learners as the guide on the side.

When we launch a math lesson, for example, learners first examine problems. Using their schema, they write down any understanding they have that relates to the problem and then begin to consider how they could solve it. After independent thinking, learners communicate ideas and thinking with their peers and build upon one another's thinking and clarify misconceptions. As a coach, I move around and engage learners in inquiry to scaffold thinking where needed and deepen understanding. I used to dominate lessons by teaching the process. Now I empower learning by allowing kids to employ their own understanding *with* support. To be clear, it is not productive for students to struggle to the point of frustration. With proper supports in place and within a culture of a growth mindset, learners feel safe to make errors and rework their strategies or thinking.

Rather than class time being consumed by my instruction of the process, we spend more time digging deeper, sharing creative ways of solving, reflecting, and creating our own problems, which engages learners in metacognition. With that said, there are times in which we need to model a process in learning; there's not a one-size-fits-all approach. Look for opportunities for learners to engage in a productive struggle, and seize them! Better yet, create them!

 Productive struggle fosters initiative, independence, personal management, persistence, help-seeking, and the ability to persist through failure.

Leveraging Technology as a Tool

Integrating technology in the classroom to accelerate learning does not require you to be an expert. While some consider our learners to be digital natives, I notice that there's a spectrum of ways that our learners harness the power of technology. Some are more tech savvy due to having families or past teachers who have exposed them to using technology as a tool to construct knowledge, design projects, or communicate with others. I also see many learners who have access to technology but predominantly use it for passive learning or entertainment.

In the same way, educators use tech for a wide variety of purposes, but supporting learners to use tech as a tool is a new concept for some teachers. If you are hesitant to teach with technology because you don't understand *everything*, take comfort in the reality you do not need to have hundreds of apps available to learners, nor do you need to understand how to use every single app fluently. Whether you are a tech expert or a complete novice, one strategy that has proven successful in my classroom is to encourage students to become "app experts" who can help their peers. Not only does this model save me time from teaching specific apps, but it also empowers learners as leaders.

As a coach, expose learners to versatile apps that empower them to demonstrate creativity, communicate their thinking, collaborate with others, and integrate Design Thinking. In our classroom, learners have access to several apps that have similar functionality. They select their preferred app based on how they want to demonstrate their thinking and then share their product with our online classroom portfolio to receive feedback. Furthermore, students are empowered to add videos and pictures of their projects, which allows them to reflect on their learning journey. Within classroom environments of empowerment, you'll observe students moving independently around the room to utilize resources and materials that support and enhance their learning. When integrating technology, leverage tools that are relevant to learners and that are likely to be used outside of school. This includes blogging, sharing documents for collaboration, providing feedback to peers through avenues such as Google Classroom (Google Docs), and developing media to enhance presentations or demonstrate learning.

Leveraging Technology as a Tool fosters initiative, independence, personal management, persistence, help-seeking, high aspirations and goal orientation, utilizing technology as a tool and the ability to persist through failure.

Choice-Infused Learning

Incorporating choice empowers learners to be intentional about selecting what works best for them. Choice is often misunderstood with teacher-created assignments that allow learners to choose which order to complete their work. While this is a starting point for providing choice, I encourage you to stretch your thinking beyond this approach.

Choice encourages learners to develop initiative due to engaging with their learning in ways that best suit their needs. In classrooms of choice, students select the strategies that work best for them and harness their strengths and interests as they decide the topic they want to learn about. Standards can always be embedded in learning; doing so simply requires that we work closely with students to ensure that they are hitting targets of learning. In our classroom, in addition to selecting their seating, students choose how to demonstrate their thinking using materials and resources of their choice. For example, in math, learners may opt to create a tutorial for peers, newscast, or artwork that incorporates concepts and strategies.

Through project-based learning and passion projects, students are empowered as the pilots of their learning as they develop driving questions or select topics that they are passionately curious to explore more deeply. Daniel Pink, author of numerous books focused on work, business, and behavior, explains what it means in terms of students having choice. He says it's about "giving them some discretion over what they study, which projects they do, what they read, or when or how they do their work—just upping the autonomy a bit. We're not talking about a wild and wooly free-for-all where everyone does whatever they want whenever they want to do it."[5] There are endless ways in which we can incorporate choice to foster the conditions for learner agency. Provide opportunities for learners to select the strategy, resources, their audience, tools to construct and demonstrate understanding, where to collaborate, and to ask questions that navigate their journey, sparking the drive to learn. From personal experiences, I notice that when we open the door to possibilities, it shifts how learners perceive school.

Likewise, author and speaker John Spencer notes, "When we incorporate choice, students own the learning process. We honor their agency and empower them to become the lifelong learners we want them to be. At some point, they will leave the classroom, and they won't have a guide right there by their side. They will have to take charge and make decisions about their own learning. This is why student choice is so critical."[6]

It's our obligation to support learners to be successful, and I don't know one teacher who disagrees. Every teacher I connect with expresses how deeply they care about their students. We need to take the L.E.A.P. and create school environments that leverage student choice to empower learning.

 Choice fosters initiative, independence, personal management, persistence, help-seeking, high aspirations and goal orientation, and utilizing technology as a tool.

Goal Setting

Early learners may struggle to grasp how to identify a reasonable goal. But even our youngest learners benefit from the goal setting process with our support. As learners practice the skill of goal setting through the years, they become empowered to determine reasonable learning targets to stretch themselves. Principal Dr. Sanée Bell explains, "Through goal setting, students become owners of their learning. Setting goals with students informs teacher practice, engages and motivates students during the learning process, and creates a partnership between the teacher, student, and parents."[7]

In my classroom, we ensure that goals are specific to each learner. While there are numerous ways to support learners in the development of goals, I utilize SMART goals.

SMART Goals

Specific (What exactly do I want to happen?)

Measurable (I will know I reached my goal when . . .)

Achievable (With hard work, is it possible to reach this goal by the deadline?)

Realistic and Relevant (I will follow this specific plan to reach my goal.)

Time bound (I will reach my goal by . . .)[8]

Learners create their plans, and I empower them to retool their plan if we recognize the need to do so. Goal setting will likely require modeling and small group or one-on-one conferencing. In our class, we post our goals to serve as a visual reminder, then conference frequently to reflect on our progress or seek help in the process. Replacing passive learning with student-created goals increases engagement and fosters learner agency.

 Goal setting fosters initiative, independence, personal management, persistence, help-seeking, high aspirations, and goal orientation as well as the ability to persist through failure.

Deep Reflection

Deep reflection empowers students to intentionally think through their learning experiences. In some scenarios, educators place reflection at the end of an activity. While there is value in that, I've found it beneficial to pause midway and allow time for students to consider what is going well as well as what needs to be improved upon. This fosters metacognition and the opportunity to immediately retool their work.

You can initiate the reflection process with students by having them think independently about what they're learning and how and why they're learning it. Students can note their reflections using a digital tool such as Google Docs, a notebook, or structured classroom protocol. In Google Docs, for example, when classmates comment on each other's work, teachers can look to see if a student chose to take the feedback provided by his peers to improve his work after reflecting on it, or if he commented back on why he elected to either keep it the same or revise it differently than suggested.

I highly recommend engaging in collaborative and peer conversations based on what learners noted or discovered in their reflection time. This gives learners the opportunity to share and show what they're working on and to offer suggestions to one another. Throughout the reflection process, I often see lightbulb moments when students make new connections to their learning. The goal is to support learners in the application of their reflections toward future work.

 Reflection fosters initiative, independence, personal management, persistence, help-seeking, high aspirations and goal orientation, and the ability to persist through failure.

L.E.A.P. Onward

Fostering the development of critical success skills in our students empowers them to be the pilots of their learning. Taking the L.E.A.P. to empower learning transforms the way we teach and the way students learn—for life. As you make shifts in your teaching style, don't be surprised if others take notice that your learners seem different, more in control of their education. Dare to continue to create the best learning opportunities for kids, while supporting them to begin developing experiences for themselves.

L.E.A.P. Tips and Takeaways

* Engage learners to initiate empowerment.
* Create opportunities for productive struggle.
* Empower learners to leverage technology as a tool.
* Provide choice to develop independent thinking.
* Support learners to set goals that are unique to their needs and passions.
* Intentionally carve out time for purposeful reflection.

L.E.A.P. beyond Your Boundaries

Share your reflections, questions, and ideas using #LEAPeffect.

1. Reflecting on student learning in your school or classroom, where would most of the day fall on the continuum of compliance, engagement, and empowerment?
2. In your school or classroom, when are learners deeply engaged in learning? How do you know they're deeply engaged?
3. What next steps will you take to empower learning or build on what you currently do?

Chapter 7
Catalyze Empowerment

I am personally convinced that one person can be a change catalyst, a 'transformer' in any situation, any organization. Such an individual is yeast that can leaven an entire loaf. It requires vision, initiative, patience, respect, persistence, courage, and faith to be a transforming leader.

—Stephen Covey

The sitcom, *Friends,* was an absolute must-watch show throughout my high school and college years. I anticipated each weekly episode and often gathered with my friends to watch the sitcom. One of my favorite episodes of all time is "The One with the Cop," which is widely known for the famed "pivot" scene. In this scene, Ross asks Rachel and Chandler to help him move his couch up the stairwell to his new apartment.

Ross makes it clear that he is in charge of the project when he shares a sketch he has drawn to map out his action plan. In a direct tone he states, "This is the way we're going to do it." Ross then directs everyone to follow his lead. The trio lifts the couch, and hilarity ensues as Ross repeatedly barks, "Pivot!" at both Rachel and Chandler as they attempt to make the turns in the stairwell. Ross's voice grows louder and more forceful as if the volume and rapid fire of words will ensure his plan is a success. With the couch firmly stuck in the stairwell and his patience tested, Chandler's frustration finally boils over and he shouts, "Shut up!" In defeat, Ross comes to the realization that his idea isn't going to work, despite having sketched out a plan.

While this scene was crafted to entertain, just imagine if the interactions and communication tactics that took place between Ross, Rachel, and Chandler occurred amongst our learners in our school or classroom. It's likely that we've witnessed learners experience a sense of struggle while striving to grasp the meaning of true collaboration, or employing effective communication strategies, where all members equally contribute ideas and are respected regardless of their opinion. I'm sure you've seen instances where one student takes charge and directs others without seeking their input. It takes practice for collaborators of any age to formulate cohesive plans, communicate effectively, and work together as they consider all of the possibilities as well as limitations.

Serve as the Catalyst

In chemistry, a catalyst serves as the spark that creates energy. The energy forms a reaction that enhances or speeds up a process. Within our learning environments, empowerment catalyzes when we infuse discussion strategies and opportunities to engage as collaborative problem *seekers*, fostering divergent thinking in a safe, classroom community which promotes responsible risk-taking. Sparking curiosity, which inspires passionate learners to be driven as problem seekers, leads us to the creation of a culture of innovation. As educators, we serve as a catalyst for our students by creating opportunities that transform the possibilities.

I'm certain that we've all heard fellow educators comment that their students don't recall what was taught earlier in the school year (possibly even a month ago) or in previous years. You may have even voiced that very concern yourself. While empowered learning has the potential to increase the likelihood that students will attain greater understanding, we have to acknowledge that learners recall information of content through relevant and meaningful learning experiences that occur within in a supportive environment. To catalyze empowerment, we must ensure that we are examining all aspects of the culture within our environment, depth of relationships, and learning structures that are employed to support each individual. Every one of these aspects of empowerment builds on previous knowledge and experience, and sometimes we must circle back and review in order to push further and learn more.

In the *Friends* episode, Chandler and Rachel weren't involved in the planning process. Ross, the dominant leader, shouted orders at his teammates instead of communicating effectively, in a positive and supportive manner. The result was an emotional outburst from Chandler, who felt frustration. Let's break this down some more. If this were our classroom, the environment would feel stressful, inhibiting divergent thinking and lessening the likelihood of our learners taking risks.

Neurologist and educator Dr. Judy Willis shares how critical a "just right" classroom environment is to support the growth of learners. In a high-stress environment or while experiencing feelings of anxiety, for example, information cannot pass through the amygdala (part of the limbic system in the temporal lobe) to develop the long-term memory of content; this is due to overstimulation of the amygdala. As educators, we need to have an awareness that stress and anxiety are often rooted in perception. Because perception is a reality to the individual experiencing it, taking the pulse of those in our classroom and being aware of the vibe we create is critical. We can create ideal conditions for learning if the environment fosters a positive emotional state layered with a stimulating amount of challenge that captivates the learners' interests.[1] Therefore, creating the "just right" classroom is not about generating an atmosphere of complete ease but one that nurtures a sense of safety amidst compelling experiences. It's in these ideal conditions that the brain activates pathways for learning and retention.

As Dr. Willis goes on to explain, research reveals that "students tested under these conditions show better working memory, improved verbal fluency, better episodic memory for events, and more flexible thinking yielding creative ideas for problem solving. They even show more positive social behaviors—helpfulness, sociability, focus, patience, and other higher-order executive function and decision-making abilities."[2]

As we craft opportunities that promote flexible thinking and creativity, we equip students as problem-solvers, which sparks the potential to foster more in-depth understanding of content leading to more significant retention. We can create a robust culture of learning through structures that catalyze empowerment. All kids deserve individuals who go to great lengths to create cultures of innovation; it doesn't have to feel like an overwhelming feat if we take steps forward together by layering opportunities for learners to develop essential success skills.

The Power of Collaborative Conversation

Whether Ross's couch actually fit or not, imagine how different the scenario could have been if all three friends were *equally* involved in sharing their ideas to transfer the sofa to Ross's new apartment. It was clear that Rachel and Chandler felt pressured to jump right in and move forward with Ross's idea rather than contribute to the planning process. As discussed in Chapter 3, relationships built on trust are the cornerstone of any successful organization and serve as the launching point for learners to take risks. When you work to establish trust between all individuals in the classroom, learners develop the confidence to share their voice.

While spending time in a second-grade classroom, I watched as the teacher engaged learners in a think-pair-share, a strategy developed for students to discuss wonderings, their understanding of a topic, affirm thinking, or access knowledge. What I noticed was one student in each pair rephrased the teacher's question to their partner. All learners demonstrated active listening, using accountable talk sentence stems. They were thoughtful in their responses and genuinely invested in conversations. The teacher rotated to groups while listening in and utilized inquiry to guide the conversation to deepen critical thinking. When learners were ready to come together and share summaries of their discussions, those listening were using hand signals to communicate to their peers and teacher visually. The teacher didn't have to redirect any student during this time, as every child was engaged and actively participating in the conversation in one way or another. Based on interactions, it was evident that learners felt safe to share their thinking and that their classroom culture nurtured positive relationships, as every child affirmed the reasoning of their peers or respectfully questioned or challenged thoughts which deepened the conversation and, in turn, the learning experience.

Let's Chat . . . to Deepen Learning

In speaking with the teacher later, she told me that she empowers students to share their ideas by providing support structures that foster the development of communication skills. You see, we want to catalyze empowerment. Students benefit from learning how to engage in conversations where they're encouraged to agree, disagree, add on to a thought, or question the thinking of their peers. Fostering communication as a skill catalyzes empowered learning along with critical thinking, as this skill easily transfers to other learning scenarios. (Regarding the hand signals that students used, they were quietly communicating with their peers and teacher that they agree, disagree, want to add on, or contribute something new to develop the conversation or learning.)

At the beginning of each year, I too start off with this strategy of supporting the development of effective communication to ensure it's purposeful. I want students to talk *with* each other rather than *at* each other. My goal is to empower them to dig deeper into their thoughts by asking questions and sharing their thinking. Often, learners feel safe sharing their ideas when talking with one or two of their peers. In our classroom, learners are always invited to share out their thinking. Meanwhile, those who are listening signal their thinking using hand gestures. Those who are less confident to speak in front of others appreciate the hand signals, as they allow sharing without stirring anxiety. In time, learners develop greater confidence as their voice grows stronger in a supportive learning environment. I have witnessed how using this strategy with learners has fostered courage within my students to not only share their thoughts but to become presenters of their learning over the course of the school year.

While this may seem like a simple strategy, learners of all ages require time to acclimate to conversation techniques if they haven't had experience. And, even if they have, learners *still benefit* from developing more in-depth conversation and speaking techniques throughout their education along with grasping how to listen with empathy and understanding. Even middle and high school students often lack the understanding of how to engage in meaningful conversations that drive thinking and deepen learning. The art of conversation benefits all learners when we intentionally hone the skills.

If you want to practice conversation and deep discussions in your classroom, consider the interests of learners and what topics might spark curiosity. No one is going to excitedly dive into a conversation that's grounded in a low-interest subject! By laying the foundation of a luminous culture, you will become more in tune with what is likely to get your students talking. From there, work to strategically develop communication skills that lead learners to take risks and actively contribute to whole-class discussions.

Empower Learners as Problem Seekers

In conversing with one of my closest friends, Beth Gibson, who is the worldwide product engineering director of Corning Incorporated, she shared that reverse innovation is shifting the way we approach and view innovative solutions. The term *reverse innovation* stirred curiosity in me. Innovation is known as the process of building or improving upon something to adapt and evolve to meet the needs of individuals. Reverse innovation, on the other hand, is the practice of taking a current product and making necessary adjustments to enhance the product's marketability in developing economies that cannot afford the models designed for the Western world. I never gave it much thought before, but numerous products we utilize don't necessarily meet the needs of those in other parts of the world. To reverse innovations, this multinational company's employees become problem *seekers* using a different lens.

If you're wondering what this concept has to do with education, consider how reverse innovation might shift how we approach learning with kids. With the focus on fostering divergent thinking and the opportunity to innovate, we need to empower learners as problem seekers. Our brains are naturally curious. When we envelop learning within problems or scenarios, it catalyzes empowerment that leads to the deepest form of learning. We then develop intrinsic motivation and synergy.

Let's explore a scenario that cultivates innovative thinking in the classroom, prior to going further with reverse innovation. One activity I use in my class that embodies innovative thinking, as we traditionally understand it, tasks learners to create a new form of wearable technology. Through inquiry, students explore the progression of wearable technology. Learners assume the role of engineer designers with the goal being to consider current, everyday problems and how wearable technology can either alleviate those problems or otherwise meet people's needs. By leveraging a variety of texts, videos, and engaging in in-depth conversations that support understanding, students use the Design Thinking process (more on Design Thinking in Part III) to craft a new or improved version of wearable technology. Activities such as these cultivate divergent thinking skills, foster agency, and are an excellent approach to developing success skills. And, although learners are empowered as problem seekers through this activity as they look to improve a product based on needs or wants, they are mainly examining inconveniences that can be made more convenient based on our Western world perspective.

Reverse innovation, on the other hand, fosters the process of identifying problems leading to the creation of innovative solutions and also promotes empathy by exposing learners to the unique needs of individuals living in developing countries. The benefit is that our learners also gain the unique perspective of those who face vastly different challenges than what we are accustomed to in our day-to-day life.

Reverse Innovation Prompts Problem Seeking

Let's explore the concept of reverse innovation to develop a better understanding of what this is in comparison to innovation as we know it. One example involves a team of designers from MIT who were charged with the task of developing a wheelchair that would perform well on rough terrain in East Africa. The wheelchairs that we are familiar with weren't a viable option for individuals in that region. The first prototype they designed was able to successfully conquer the rough terrain, but it had to be retooled because it was unable to fit through doorways.

Designers understood that creating a model that solved one existing problem wasn't enough. They had to consider all of the possible issues that may exist with each redesign. They then tested the product in the field in real-world conditions. In doing so, designers were able to evaluate the effectiveness of their design and seek out other potential problems that should influence their final design.

In the classroom, we need to support learners to embrace the understanding that, "design is iterative; you can't get it right the first time, so be prepared to test many prototypes."[3] Learning experiences within STEAM challenges or problem- and project-based learning often provide students with constraints to work within. Constraints can lead to more significant creative thinking, as learners are encouraged to identify ways to innovate inside the box. I employ an assortment of structures throughout the school year to expose learners to a wide variety of learning experiences that include STEAM challenges as well as problem- and project-based learning. To catalyze empowerment through problem seeking, we can blend in the practice of reverse innovation, too.

Here are a few questions you can pose to foster divergent thinking and catalyze empowerment:

* What do you wonder?
* What more do we need to know?
* How will we locate the information?
* What materials do we require?
* How can we best improve our designs?
* How do you want to monitor, track, and demonstrate your learning journey?
* What does success look like to you?

Invite learners to examine specific products that they're accustomed to seeing or using and then explore the value of those products in a third-world country. Within learning, we can layer new information about the product, clients, or the environment in which they live. The idea that one product may be conducive with the terrain (as in the example from MIT) but now won't suffice in the home encourages learners to look at a design from all angles and gather more information to drive the learning process. Learners should also consider if the parts to build it would be available in that country and how to make the cost of manufacturing affordable.

Brief Detour

Let's take a detour and go off track for a moment. In my experiences working with educators, and as a classroom teacher myself, I know that we agonize over the amount of time we have and how we will possibly thoroughly cover all of the standards and content we're expected to teach. I want to validate your feelings connected to these pressures. As educators, these constraints will always exist. I cannot create more time in your day, but I am confident that by embedding learning standards into the experiences you facilitate, you will create the time you need while also catalyzing empowerment.

Learning must be meaningful and impactful. When we craft learning experiences that are interdisciplinary, multiple standards are incorporated. In the example I provided above, you could integrate English language arts, science, technology, engineering, math, social studies, and art. By creating opportunities for learners to develop the ability to seek problems and create unique solutions *while* embedding standards, we can ensure optimum learning for all and cultivate future success skills.

Choice, Creativity, and Student Agency

While collaboratively working on a complex math problem set in a real-world context, children in my class selected the app they wanted to use to record their thinking and solving processes. With the iPad placed in front of them, learners recorded themselves reading the problem and discussing their wonderings, along with each step of their thinking associated with the problem. During this activity, one student, Susie, stopped the recording abruptly and exclaimed, "I accidentally did all of the talking, and didn't mean to do so! No one had the opportunity to agree or disagree with me, let alone add on! Let's restart and be sure to share why we agree, disagree, and show our thinking." Her team members agreed, and they restarted. It's moments like this that bring a smile to my face. Unlike Ross in the *Friends* episode, Susie caught herself, naturally reflected, then retooled to ensure all voices were involved.

While the first recording seemed to lack pizzazz, personalities blossomed in the second take as learners began to accentuate the way they read the story problem and even assumed the role of reporters by turning to team members to interview them for input. Not once did

I have to interfere with their project by redirecting. Each team would review their recording and make appropriate adjustments based on their reflective conversations. In addition to reflecting, these children were collaborating, providing feedback, revising, and demonstrating complete agency over the learning process and how they brought the product together. With the opportunity to release creativity and playfulness, joy in learning unfolded and the synergy was palpable. Culture in combination with empowering choice and creativity catalyzes the power to create opportunities that elevate retention of learning and boost divergent thinking.

Engaging students in relevant, complex problem-solving and leveraging tech tools that allow for the creation of videos or other creative means to capture learning dynamically goes beyond merely applying math standards. The intent is to identify how we can infuse voice, choice, and creativity as well as the components we hit on in Chapter 6, including productive struggle, leveraging technology as a tool, goal setting, and reflection.

Reflection and Revision

Reflection is a critical skill we can cultivate to great depths to support learners in gaining insight into their thinking and monitor understanding. Placing an intentional emphasis on reflection lends itself to greater confidence amongst learners as they recognize that each person thinks differently, thus fostering divergent thinking and provoking creativity. To jumpstart the process of reflection in our class, students start by posting their thinking on our "thought wall." Our wall is broken into multiple sections to allow for visible thinking. At the start of an activity, learners post a sticky note stating what they notice or any connections they recognize relating to a problem or whatever it is they're reviewing. (It could be an article, experiment, graphic, etc.). After further review, they post a sticky note that documents their predictions in addition to initial questions based on their curiosities. Using math as an example, learners pause after breaking apart and solving a problem using one strategy, reflect on their learning, and then post any new findings, connections, or predictions of how others may have solved the problem or questions that they have about the concept. Finally, they revisit this process as they begin to wrap up their work. Throughout this activity, learners are able to revise their work as they pause to take their thinking, or that of their peers, into consideration.

Metacognition deepens as learners are immersed in the process of reflection and revision. Rather than solely completing assignments for finality, they become actively engaged in their thought processes and develop agency as thinkers and learners. From the educator's perspective, we acquire a unique glimpse into the thinking of each student to personalize our approach to best support their learning. As learners read the reflections of others, they begin asking new questions to seek understanding and gain the perspective of their peers. Through reflection, a community of learners emerges as they explore, question, and link ideas together to reframe thinking or create new concepts.

L.E.A.P. Onward

Ideally, I want students to feel empowered right from the start of each school year. My hope is that they will learn to engage in fruitful and reflective conversations that deepen learning as described. It takes time, practice, and patience for us to get to that point. By setting the stage early on, we can generate agency through fostering choice and creativity in learning by listening to how our students want to demonstrate their understanding—rather than us placing parameters on how they do so. That's not to say that we shouldn't ever provide guidelines or expectations; in fact, constraints often lead to divergent thinking as they may prompt individuals to innovate within the box. If guidelines tightly rule the daily occurrences in our classrooms, however, we may unintentionally create conditions that lead to passive learning.

If passive learning is what your students are accustomed to, start the conversation by engaging in whole-class discussions to create a list of options that exist to capture and exhibit thinking or learning. Once learners understand and believe that their voice is valued in your classroom, they will be more likely to share ideas that you may have never before considered, taking their education further than ever imagined.

L.E.A.P. Tips and Takeaways

* Create resources that serve as visuals to support learners with talking stems for accountable talk.
* Intentionally practice accountable talk using high-interest or thought-provoking content.

* Within a culture that supports risk-taking, encourage learners to respectfully question their peers and share thoughts, ideas, and opinions.
* Empower learners to ask purposeful questions as problem seekers and keep record of their wonderings.
* Create authentic, meaningful education by incorporating interdisciplinary learning that integrates multiple standards.
* Leverage technology as a creative tool for students to demonstrate thinking and learning to aid in reflection and revision.

L.E.A.P. beyond Your Boundaries

Share your reflections, questions, and ideas using #LEAPeffect.

1. How can you enhance communication between learners to deepen thinking?
2. What authentic problems exist that are relevant to your learners?
3. How can you facilitate learning to support students in beginning to identify problems that exist?
4. What are some ways you can employ deeper reflection to lead to refined revisions at various grade levels?

Chapter 8
Spark Motivation to Learn

Our chief want is someone who will inspire
us to be what we know we could be.

—Ralph Waldo Emerson

Exhausted after an extra-long workday, I mindlessly scrolled through my social media feed as I left my school building. Rather than going out my normal exit, I chose another one nearby for no particular reason. Upon opening the door, the brisk wind smacked me in the face, and I couldn't help but feel somewhat disgruntled between the bite of the cold and that there was no time to relax between work and returning home to prepare dinner. It had been a day where it felt like the odds were against me. From around the corner, I heard the voices of boys, but engrossed in my feed, I didn't look up as I passed by. Out of the corner of my eye, I saw a blond-haired boy wave and then call out, "Hey, Mrs. Bostwick!"

Briefly, I glanced at the boy, said, "Hi," and returned to scrolling. Suddenly, I did a double take, and it hit me that the boy was a former second-grade student of mine from nine years prior. I spun back around and said, "Jason! I didn't even recognize you at first! How are you?"

"Good. I'm doing good," he said.

I smiled. "That's great, it's wonderful to see you, enjoy your evening!" I said and then turned to continue walking toward my car.

Even though our brief conversation appeared cordial, the exchange was not typical for me, as thoughts of what I needed to accomplish in a short amount of time consumed my thoughts. I should have paused to talk more with Jason, and in my mind I justified rushing off by thinking that a teenager wouldn't want to catch up with his teacher from second grade. I was wrong. What happened next continues to influence the way I approach *every interaction I have with others.*

Almost a Missed Opportunity

Suddenly, Jason yelled, "Actually, Mrs. Bostwick, I'm not good at all." At that moment, my brain snapped back to reality. My eyes met his, and based on his expression, I could tell he felt distraught.

"What's going on?" I asked as I walked back toward him.

Jason confided that he was frustrated with school. His perception was that his teachers didn't really care about him and that school seemed pointless. He told me that he felt like a failure because he was not doing well in any subject area.

Hearing this pained my heart. I remembered Jason as a vibrant seven-year-old, full of curiosity and ingenuity. After listening to him express his feelings, I said, "I'm so sorry to hear," then proceeded to share, "You may not believe this, but I experienced my own struggles in school." I could tell this took him by surprise, so I elaborated, sharing a piece of my story and how I had a handful of educators in my life who served as a source of inspiration to me. Most kids don't view teachers as people who have faced difficulties related to education, but I shared that I'm in the field of education today because I am determined to be an agent of change. My driving force is to bring the very best learning opportunities to kids while helping them to comprehend that their voice matters. I then asked, "What are you passionate about?" Jason cocked his head to the side as if he'd never been asked that before. And, most likely, he hadn't. I reframed the question, "What interests you?"

After some thought, Jason responded with, "Well, I'm interested in cooking and have thought about becoming a chef." He went on to tell me about the dishes he enjoyed making, His face lit up when talking about cooking!

I listened and encouraged him to be intentional about identifying his interests and strengths. I explained that understanding his passions might make learning more meaningful. "That's not to say every day will feel exciting or purposeful," I warned him. "But we need to keep our eyes focused on our goals and what we need to do to reach them. Embedding our passions into whatever it is that we're doing can inspire us to persevere through challenging times and find fulfillment in life."

Often, we talk about following or finding our passions. The reality is that many kids, and even adults, aren't sure what they're passionate about or how it connects to their life, particularly if they haven't had exposure to various topics or a wealth of experiences. Perhaps they haven't yet discovered their interests. Our focus ought to be on exposing learners to a variety of experiences and encouraging them to identify their unique interests, leading to the development of passions; it empowers. It's important for students to have an awareness that passions begin as interests and are developed over time. In Part

III, helping to develop learners' interests will be our primary focus as we explore ways to embrace a maker culture, infuse passions, and integrate elements of project-based learning to create authentic experiences. Passions are likely to change over time, which is why exposure to various subjects beyond what we traditionally highlight in school is critical. We must support learners by developing a culture where everyone is open to exploring new interests, with the understanding that learning requires grit too. Just because a child is interested or even passionate about a topic does not mean that understanding will come easily.

Research shows that when something feels difficult, it may send the message that the topic is not of interest. In reality, if we encourage students to persist and thereby cultivate a growth mindset and allow for incremental success, students will learn by experience that they can overcome challenges. The more frequently they persist and experience learning "wins," the more they *want* to persevere through difficulties. It's a cycle that promotes growth and the development of new interests.[1]

I am certainly passionate about education, but there are days that are enjoyable and others that are downright challenging. Because I'm passionate about my work and driven to be a positive force of influence, the thought of quitting doesn't cross my mind—which is where Jason was mentally when we spoke that day outside my school.

As educators, we are the influencers who can inspire learners to persevere through difficult situations. We do that by nurturing a supportive environment where relationships flourish, students pursue their interests, and they feel confident that they won't be penalized. These environments drive us all to spend our time and energy learning anything new. They are what make students feel invested in their education. And when combined, relationships and relevancy have the power to unlock amazing potential in our learners—and ourselves.

Jason seemed desperate for genuine relationships and relevancy in his learning, and he wasn't getting it in the classroom. So, during our conversation, I told him about a few terrific programs available within our region provided to our school district, which support learners who want to acquire culinary skills. We discussed that sometimes school isn't going to be what we had hoped, but it's not a reason to walk away from education. We all need to find our niche and connect with the right people. But because that is easier said than done, I encouraged him to remain in school—to stick it out—even as he pursued other avenues that enabled him to connect with his interests.

As we wrapped up our conversation, Jason smiled broadly and reached out to give me a fist bump. "That's exactly what I needed to hear, thank you! I never thought about the fact that there are possibilities beyond what I see at the moment," he said. "I was starting to feel like quitting was my only option. You always just 'got us,' as our teacher."

Wow. In that moment, Jason affirmed me by acknowledging one of the many reasons I went into education. During our conversation, I was cognizant to listen and validate, demonstrate vulnerability, and use guiding questions to help Jason consider what he's interested in to relate back to the purpose of his education. My hope is that the next time I speak with Jason, I'll find that he continued to actively pursue a path that's right for him.

On the car ride home, I thought about all the things that occurred to make that moment happen, starting with my late departure. If I'd left earlier, Jason and I wouldn't have crossed paths. And I never would have passed by him if I'd exited my usual way. If we hadn't developed a relationship in my class years earlier, he would never have reached out for help.

In our schools we need to be intentional about the steps we're taking to influence our learners as we seek to empower them to take ownership of their learning. And when moments for influence happen by "coincidence," we have to make the most of them.

Seize Opportunities to Influence

One of our most important roles as educators is that of influencer. Each of us has influence, and the kind of influence we have—be it positive or negative—is within our control. It's so easy to get caught up in day-to-day routines, but pausing to reflect on the way we choose to influence others is an invaluable practice. Because for every kid like Jason who reaches out for help, there are one hundred more who may never speak up, even though they need our intention and attention. Those kids don't need us to push them in a particular standardized direction. What they need is for us to help them identify their strengths and interests. By exposing them to various learning experiences, they discover what they love and learn to embrace their unique gifts—and those of others. In that kind of luminous culture, robust, relevant learning occurs, which pushes them to contribute their best.

Identifying Strengths

I don't want to just breeze by this concept of helping students find their strengths. We can serve as a positive force of influence by highlighting the strengths of learners and providing space for them to leverage and apply their abilities. By empowering our learners to discover what they can do for themselves and to seek opportunities to expand their learning, we demonstrate our belief in them. I like to use resources such as Thrively.com, which assists learners in identifying their strengths and uncovering their interests. This tool can also help you recognize strengths in learners that you may not have noticed.

When I first explored Thrively, I had my son Nolan answer the questions designed for students to see just how accurate the results would be. Boy, were they spot on! Nolan was classified as an Analyst Extraordinaire. Listed as his top strengths were assertiveness, verbal, leadership, and analytical. These are, in fact, many of the strengths that his exceptional and influential fourth-grade teacher, Miss. Shutter, recognized in him, highlighted, and shared with us. In Nolan's words, "She's the best teacher I've ever had; she liked me for me."

Kids know when we value them; they're way more perceptive that we realize. Looking back, I see that Nolan's teacher tapped into his abilities and grasped how to help navigate them in order to do his personal best. Something I found interesting, when looking at Nolan's strengths, is that although our society appreciates adults who exhibit assertiveness and leadership skills, schools tend to frown upon the same strengths in children. Those very strengths, however, could help Nolan be successful during and beyond school. The lesson here is that, if we expect compliance but have students who are naturally strong in assertiveness and leadership, their personalities may not jive with our expectations. But when we identify how to leverage natural abilities, we influence learners to use their strengths appropriately.

In addition to Thrively.com, I also use the framework of Ignite Your S.H.I.N.E.®, created by LaVonna Roth. This program helps individuals identify their strengths, gifts, and passions, with the focus on one's exceptional self in order to serve others better. My learners and I have reaped the benefits of integrating the framework in the classroom, and it's precisely the kind of exploration that Jason needed. As learners reveal and embrace their shine—S.H.I.N.E. stands for Self-Heart-Inspire-Navigate-Exceptional—they realize that they have strengths, talents, and passions that uniquely contribute to navigating their journey as the most exceptional version of themselves. As they grow more confident in how they shine, they develop greater courage to take risks. In a culture where everyone is encouraged to shine, learners feel self-assured as divergent thinkers and leaders.

Journeying through the lessons within the framework with my students, I've watched them blossom and truly thrive in who they are as individuals, embrace their peers, and demonstrate vulnerability, in addition to originality.

Captivate Learners through the Influence of Trends

Cultivating a joy in learning can also be inspired by infusing pop-culture trends and empowering our youth to put their original spin on learning. After all, it's yet another strategy that increases engagement, leading to learner agency. As this happens, a true personalization of learning can occur as we draw on the interests of learners and connect it to content. (For clarity's sake, it's important to note that personalization of learning varies from personalized learning. Whereas personalized learning is when each learner has a distinct pathway, often provided through technology, personalization of learning incorporates and builds upon learners' interests to create engaging and meaningful learning opportunities.)[2] Furthermore, when we leverage current interests of learners and have full engagement, we can foster greater levels of grit in them as well.

From the Rainbow Loom® to Fidget Spinners, pop culture trends have a powerful pull for our youth. When the latest and greatest fad hits the market, kids go wild trying to attain it. I recall when my own boys yearned for every color of mini rubber bands to create another bracelet with the Rainbow Loom. They sought out YouTube channels dedicated to creating new designs and would rewind video clips until they mastered the next step and figured out how to craft the design they wanted. A few years down the road, our son Julian was an early adopter with the fidget spinner trend—a mere three weeks later, it became all the rave in the elementary buildings. It began showing up across social media as people expressed feelings of either delight or dreadfulness. Kids weren't simply spinning the gadget; they were challenging one another to different spinning techniques, spinning on one finger or trying to hold steady as it spun on their nose, and so on.

Industries are constantly innovating and creating new, catchy trends to captivate kids' attention. Rather than bucking these pop-culture trends and competing with them for our students' attention, many educators have learned to leverage them as opportunities to incorporate them into the classroom. Rainbow Looms, for example, have been spotted in makerspaces and classroom creation stations to foster fine motor skills, listening skills (YouTube tutorials), and even critical thinking as students work out how to master complex designs. Some educators invite learners to go a step further and create their own videos demonstrating the steps to craft their unique designs.

As for fidget spinners, well, just make a quick visit to TeachersPayTeachers.com and you'll find 1,279 results (and counting) of activities using these gadgets for everything from practicing math facts and speech to STEAM challenges and more. Educators recognize the value of integrating pop-culture trends and are innovating the way they teach to influence learners to *want* to learn. Some might say, "If you can't beat them, you might as well join them," but I believe that relationships are reciprocal, and understanding our students and their interests provides an opportunity to develop and incorporate personalization of learning. When we make learning relevant by connecting to their "real world" (aka life outside of school) they are more likely to see *school* as empowering and meaningful. Might I add a brief side note, though, that just because an activity taps into a trend and creates high engagement, as teachers, we are still responsible for ensuring that the learning taking place meets the ultimate goal of empowering learners within a culture of innovation.

Fascinatingly, with each new fad, kids seek and even develop varying levels of challenges to conquer. Take water bottle flipping, for example. I was impressed at how tenacious kids were at flipping to land their bottle just so. I watched them launch a bottle over and over until they landed it correctly, only to do it again. Some, like my son Julian, began to analyze the amount of water in the bottle to get the "perfect landing." When kids conquered one challenge, they'd increase the level of difficulty by creating a new test for their skills. Whatever the challenge, kids are willing to practice for hours on end to achieve each new goal. Now think about this: *Are learners actively creating challenges and seeking to overcome them to achieve their goals demonstrating dedication to learning in school?*

In the spring of 2018, Fortnite took our world by storm as a free-to-play video game. It's currently the fastest growing game, yielding $300 million per month from optional purchases—people of all ages, genders, and nationalities have Fortnite fever! You may wonder what makes this game so wildly popular. According to video game expert Joost Van Dreunen, CEO of Superdata, the reason Fortnite hit over 100 million users in July 2018 and is said to pull in over $300 million per month is because people are drawn to the colorful, cartoony graphics, humor, and interactions between characters.[3] The competition, strategy, continuous novelty, and collaboration all contribute to the game's appeal, as does the less-serious "playground mode" that gives players free reign to build, talk with peers, and have their characters dance or try new challenges. Understanding what captivates gamers is valuable to us in education.

I've watched my own two boys become hooked on Fortnite. They enjoy that it allows them to imagine, create, and engage in iteration of ideas. Playing with relentless determination and intense collaboration, they strive to reach new levels of achievement. When my kids "fail" at the game, they don't give up; they jump right back in with even greater determination than before. They demonstrate the kind of grit teachers long to see in students at school. From our kitchen, I can hear our boys excitedly interacting and communicating with teammates. Never once have I had to remind them to focus on the game or prompt them to spend more time playing. Rather, I find myself regulating their game time to ensure they have balance. Even so, their level of dedication and grit makes me curious about what we could be doing to inspire those traits in the classroom.

Kids actively seek out challenges and are driven to accomplish what they're focused on, particularly when they're highly interested in a topic—and that truth isn't relegated to video games and water bottle flips. At a regional STEAM conference, several middle schoolers were assigned to help with my session, which included coding robotics to demonstrate learning possibilities within maker education. While we worked to prepare for the presentation, I wondered how my helpers felt about school. "What do you enjoy most about school?" I asked. Their responses ranged from lunch to passing between classes. *Yikes!*

As we continued to talk, these middle school students explained that, although they had a background in coding due to camps they had attended, they lacked the advanced supplies that I had on hand that day at the conference. One girl said, "You know, I think school would be more interesting if we could use robotics and materials to create in our classes."

Of course, we all have different budgets and structures, but I know that we *can* craft relevant, engaging, and empowering learning experiences for kids, even without expensive or elaborate resources. In Part III, we'll explore how we can also support learners to create these opportunities for themselves—in other words, developing another pathway to empower learning.

Creating Relevancy

Denis Sheeran, director of student achievement and author of *Instant Relevance* and *Hacking Mathematics*, hosted a Twitter chat on #MakeItReal, discussing ways to leverage Fortnite in the classroom. Now, let me preface with the fact that I'm not necessarily promoting that we use video games themselves, but the concept of incorporating gaming themes and design can be a powerful way to spark students' motivation to learn.

In the compilation of the chat, which can be read in its entirety on Participate.com, we can gain insight on the concept. Launching the chat with the first question, Sheeran asked participants to share how they're using Fortnite as part of learning in the classroom. I was impressed with what followed! Various educators shared that they use the concept of Fortnite to connect to distance formula, circumference, and many other topics within mathematics and physics. A Spanish teacher shared, too, that she empowered learners to create a slideshow of a town of their choice found within Fortnite, compose a paragraph, and then label each place in Spanish.[4]

On social media, countless educators are seeking to create relevant learning experiences that connect to the interests of students. We can select just about any topic and find tips or strategies, including escape rooms and Breakout EDU, that incorporate academic content or ideas to gamify learning, elevating engagement to catapult us to empowerment.

Gaming Design Elevates Learning

If we take a step back and analyze gaming design, we gain a better understanding of why video gaming itself is so captivating. Video games, which are designed to be fun and provide incremental success, trigger the brain to release higher rates of dopamine, a neurotransmitter that sends signals to other nerve cells. Dopamine causes a pleasurable effect in response to making predictions and plays a significant role in motivating humans. Ultimately, it's the release of dopamine that creates the desire within individuals to continuously return to the game, sparking intrinsic motivation to embrace challenges and move toward the goal. Children require more frequent boosts of dopamine, as opposed to adults, to sustain focus and persevere through challenges.[5]

Understanding how the brain responds to gaming provides educators with invaluable information on how we can spark our students' motivation to learn. And if we focus on the elements of game design, not video games themselves, we can find ways to leverage the powerful effect that challenging play has on the brain.

The Elements of Game Design that Elevate Engagement and Drive Learning

Relevance to Learners

When students perceive something as relevant, they desire to learn and know more. Video games and their themes are tailored for targeted audiences and designed to capture that specific audience's full attention. Think *ultimate engagement*. Whether it be the storyline, characters, or challenges, learners connect to the premise of the game. Games are filled with novelty and discovery; they are created to stir curiosity and pull in players. The best games provide choice—in avatars, actions, player modes, and play (solo or collaborative). In Fortnite, for example, learners have the option to compete independently, collaborate with a team, or enter playground mode to build and design. These choices give them the autonomy to create their own experiences.

A Balance of Challenge and Perceived Skill

As kids engage in video gaming, they make predictions on what to do next to achieve a challenge. This may entail an action, choice or prediction, and even input from their peers. If what they do is correct, they advance to the next level—and receive another boost of dopamine. The challenge and reward process fuels the brain to continue working toward the next achievement. Every time they reach success, they're motivated to continue trying repeatedly. For optimum engagement, the level of challenge and perceived skill must be balanced. Tracy Fullerton, author of *Game Design Workshop: A Playcentric Approach to Designing Innovative Games,* explains, "If the level of challenge remains appropriate to the level of ability, and if this challenge rises as the ability level rises, the person will stay in the center region and experience . . . 'flow.' In flow, an activity balances a person between challenge and ability, frustration and boredom, to produce an experience of achievement and happiness."[6]

Incremental and Intuitive Success

Video games provide incremental success by allowing players to advance to new levels, but never at a rate quicker than what they can master. With deep determination, kids will attack challenges until they reach success, only to persist to the next level. Interestingly, while playing video games, kids face failure *80 percent of the time,*[7] but because they receive feedback that they're gradually reaching their goal—they can see their progress and experience moments of success—they continue to persist in the face of challenge. In Super Mario Bros., gamers can see all of the worlds that lie ahead awaiting to be unlocked and explored. They have an idea what the challenges before them may be, and they know where they'll end up. But until they begin, they're not certain how to conquer the upcoming challenges.

Immediate Feedback

The immediate feedback players receive while playing entices them to continue pushing forward. They instinctively learn to make predictions based on past performance indicators that signal how to improve during the next attempt. Despite the fact that there is no tangible trophy or formal awards ceremony where families gather, they persevere forward with feedback in the form of chimes, graphic displays, power-ups, coins, or new digital tools and even outfits for their avatars. Every bit of feedback the brain receives reinforces networks of memory used to predict success.[8]

When my husband and I purchased Super Mario Bros. for our boys, we didn't sit down with a manual or instruct our boys on how to use the controllers or what to do in the first level. We simply provided the freedom for them to explore and learn by doing. (I suppose we took somewhat of a constructivist approach with video gaming, if that's a thing.) Our boys engaged in a productive struggle as they faced challenges and worked to overcome them through trial and error. They used feedback from the game to adjust their approach and retool their technique, and they successfully unlocked all the lands over time.

Identity, Personalization, and Sense of Connectedness

From Minecraft to Fortnite, learners create their own identities based on their interests and how they want to be perceived by others. They build their own dwellings and can wear "skins" to communicate their personality. Although kids often desire to connect and have friendships based on interests and commonalities, they also enjoy showcasing their originality in the "safety" of the gaming world, as it's customizable on demand. Through gaming, they also develop a sense of connectedness through partnering on missions or creating worlds with their imaginations. Connectedness fosters a sense of community and belonging and develops the foundation for communication leading to new ideas.[9,10]

In learning, we can infuse elements of game design in the following ways:

* Providing choice
* Facilitating with inquiry
* Promoting collaboration and effective communication
* Empowering learners to pinpoint relevant topics, challenges, or problems that exist
* Inviting discovery through exploration
* Fostering a culture that embraces a growth mindset
* Leveraging the strengths of learners
* Engaging learners in productive struggle
* Ensuring that learners receive both independent and small group support at a level of growth
* Developing a plan for goal setting, monitoring, and celebration of all levels of success
* Employing tools that allow for immediate feedback
* Empowering learners to demonstrate their learning, leveraging their strengths and creativity

Reflecting on what we've explored in Part II, we can see everything from relationships to engagement, empowerment, relevance, communication, and more embedded here in the elements of game design. Within Part III, we'll look at how we can empower learners through authentic experiences connecting learners with interests.

I wonder how Jason's perception of school—or even that of the middle schoolers who assisted me in my presentation—could have been different if his teachers intentionally made connections to students' interests and integrated elements of gaming design? As educators, we must be aware of our focus: Is it on the content we need to cover? Or do we focus on creating experiences that draw kids in and sparking motivation to *want* to learn? We need to demonstrate to learners that their interests matter and that what they enjoy outside of school can connect with their learning. Although we certainly don't need to jump on every trend that emerges, we *should* seek out opportunities to elevate motivation whenever possible to encourage the journey toward empowerment.

L.E.A.P. Onward

People of all ages thrive when the influencers in their lives explicitly say, "I care about who you are as an individual as well as your interests." As influencers ourselves, we can connect with our learners and demonstrate our belief in them by recognizing and honoring their strengths and appreciating who they are rather than trying to mold them into who we feel they should be. We can spark their motivation to learn by incorporating their interests in the classroom and fostering empowerment.

Creating novel experiences that leverage the interests of students can take more time than simply sticking to the traditional approaches, but the payoff is worth every ounce of effort. As discussed earlier, research suggests that superior learning takes place when classroom experiences are enjoyable and relevant to students' lives, interests, and experiences. As we move into the next section, we'll explore how we can bring authentic learning experiences to the forefront of the classroom and how we can provide room for learners to create these opportunities for themselves—through maker education, passion projects, and project-based learning.

L.E.A.P. Tips and Takeaways

* Avoid stereotyping kids. Every child has unique strengths; seek them out.
* Encourage and provide opportunities for learners to both identify and leverage their strengths.
* Invest time listening to the interests of learners and remain cognizant of what's new in pop culture.
* Create themed lessons or units connecting to the interests of learners to integrate novelty, an element of fun, and collaboration, thus increasing engagement.
* Allow choice in the content of learning while developing skills (e.g., Minecraft math challenges and incorporating gaming fundamentals).
* Leverage the elements of video game design to increase intrinsic motivation.

L.E.A.P. beyond Your Boundaries

Share your reflections, questions, and ideas using #LEAPeffect.

1. How might helping a learner to recognize his or her interests, along with strengths, be a game changer?
2. What is one lesson you currently teach that you could begin integrating the interests of learners or elements of game design?

Part III
Authenticity in Learning

Chapter 9
Embracing a Maker Culture

The world as we have created it is a
process of our thinking. It cannot be
changed without changing our thinking.

—Albert Einstein

My imagination ran wild in the forts my neighborhood friends and I built in the wooded areas nearby. Using sticks, rocks, and anything else we could find, we'd design elaborate forest homes. Our limited materials sparked a practice of iteration, and, through creative flow, we began to imagine available resources in new ways. If our parents had visited, they might have only been able to see our space for what it looked like; but we saw magnificent rooms in an imaginary home that I'm certain looked different to each of us. We had a blast dreaming up design plans and collaborating to make our vision come to fruition.

Our neighborhood was lively with young kids, and we spent our time together after school and throughout the summers creating new games, unique inventions, and recording skits using my family's enormous '80s-style video recorder that required VHS cassette tapes. Those moments created some of the best memories of my childhood. Looking back, we all embraced a maker mindset without really knowing that's what it was. No one taught or told us what to make or create; it's just what we did for fun. If you grew up in a pre-video-game world, or even a time when electronic devices were not as accessible, you can probably relate to those experiences.

Making is not a new concept, and if you take a look at social media or do an internet search for "maker education," you'll see it in action in schools around the world. The maker movement is built upon the foundation of constructivism, brought to light by Jean Piaget. The constructivist learning theory teaches that individuals acquire knowledge through experiences, personal background knowledge, and making connections through both.

Making is most effective in education when intentionally personalized for learners; it should not be confused with culminating projects. Ideally, learners should be provided autonomy through active learning opportunities to construct their own knowledge. In other words, the final product is less important than the experience and challenge of making it.

How to Foster a Maker Culture

Some schools have fully funded and well-stocked makerspaces, complete with the latest and greatest technologies. The spaces themselves may even be flashy with the most beautiful and innovative room designs. Trust me when I say that maker education does not require you to have to have the most impressive technology or even a room dedicated as the makerspace, although both certainly have unique advantages. Instead of high-tech gadgets, students often use cardboard, batteries, paper towel tubes, empty spools, and a bit of wiring, string, tape, or whatever other random supplies are donated or rescued from the recycling bin. To innovate within the box, many schools use carts or large rolling bookshelves loaded with bins full of materials for making; the makerspace then travels from room to room. The point is that the supplies and space itself are not the most important part of fostering a maker culture.

The most advantageous makerspaces infuse students' interests, curiosities, and passions. These spaces are set up to intentionally provide opportunities for exploration, creativity, critical thinking, and collaboration.

I've spoken with many educators who have expressed feelings of insecurity because they don't know how to use all of the resources available in their schools' makerspaces. I tell them that's okay—and normal! You can learn a lot by exploring alongside students. I've learned just as much as my students while making, if not more, as they've learned from me.

Early on in my maker education experiences, I observed students expressing frustration or feeling uncomfortable exploring, making, or creating without formal direction. I attribute it in part to the convergent thinking that dominates our current standards-driven education system, where learners are seeking one "right" approach or answer, as opposed to remaining open to multiple possible solutions when immersed in divergent thinking approaches. If our schools focus more on compliance-based thinking, we might inadvertently inhibit open play or maker experiences, which foster divergent thinking, enhancing creativity.

Just like students, educators who are accustomed to direct instruction as the primary avenue to facilitate learning may feel awkward transitioning to student-led or student-centered learning. By cultivating the maker mindset—in our students and ourselves—we can integrate making in a way that enhances learning as part of the natural flow of education, rather than segregating it as an activity separate from other content areas.

When I consider integrating maker education into a subject area, I focus on two questions:

1. What is the goal or focus of learning?
2. What skills do I want to develop in my learners?

We know that maker education can encapsulate creative design and expression utilizing high-tech resources (robotics, 3D printing, coding, etc.), along with commonly found household items. Also included in maker education is video creation using green screens and editing software, art that depicts learning or that serves as a visual representation, and even the production of skits to communicate or summarize learning. For example, in English Language Arts, learners could develop a newscast where they assume the roles of characters from a text and engage in interactive interviews with a news anchor, describing what caused their character(s) to change from the beginning to the end of a story. Or, in social studies, digital media can be leveraged to create podcasts that incorporate a compilation of information on a topic of focus, embedding learning standards and targets. Rather than making a diorama to depict the Civil War Era, we can foster divergent thinking and more in-depth learning by asking, "What kind of technological device could you create to assist individuals of the past in the Civil War Era, using what you know today." Learners can select who the device is for, why it would have been beneficial, and how the device would work. Within a project like this, various learning standards from ELA, social studies, and writing can be embedded. When we talk about "making," we have to remember that making can take on many forms.

After delivering a presentation at the NYSCATE (New York State Curriculum for Advanced Technological Education) conference, I was approached by several educators who openly shared their fears about maker education. They wanted greater understanding as they contemplated taking the L.E.A.P. Maybe you have some of the same fears or questions they did:

* What if it's chaotic?
* Could it result in lost instruction time?
* What are the main benefits when purposefully developed?

These are all valid concerns, and it's natural to question change when we're uncertain about how to navigate within constraints. The good news is that when it comes down to it, *every* child is a maker by nature. We don't need to teach students to be makers; we need to sustain (or perhaps revive) their natural sense of curiosity by providing outlets for creativity that foster innovation. If our schools have fallen prey to fostering convergent thinking in place of divergent thinking skills, learners will likely need their teachers to scaffold experiences that intentionally inspire creativity and wonder. The Design Thinking process, for example, is an approach that supports learners in structuring their maker time so that they are able to show the evolution of their thinking while remaining on track with their original question.

The way to overcome the common fears or concerns regarding maker education is to dive in! I've heard from so many educators who have said that the answers to their questions became evident in the process of fostering a culture of making. So don't wait until you know everything or have the whole process figured out—because there is no finality to the process. Maker education is a way of thinking that continues to expand through various authentic learning experiences.

The current culture of your school and how much voice and choice are already empowered in learning will influence the efficiency of the process. But I think you'll find that when you develop a culture of making, classroom-management issues will decrease. At the same time, authentic instruction will increase when making is integrated in content.

A culture of making is essential to equipping learners as divergent thinkers who are empowered to consider various solutions to problems or dream up new ideas. Dale Dougherty, founder of *MAKE Magazine* and creator of Maker Faire, sums up the importance of cultivating the maker mindset to enhance culture:

> Fostering the maker mindset through education is a fundamentally human project—to support the growth and development of another person not just physically, but mentally and emotionally. Learning should focus on the whole person because any truly creative enterprise requires all of us, not just some part. It should also be rooted in the kind of sharing of knowledge and skills that humans do best face to face.[1]

Maker education is for every person. It allows us the opportunity to expose learners to a variety of experiences and topics. As I mentioned in the previous chapter, by helping students explore existing interests or discover new fascinations, we can also help them identify and develop their passions. Exploration through maker education may lead students to connect with interests they may have never otherwise considered. Every child deserves the opportunity to explore their curiosities and develop skills.

"Your Idea Is Too Big,"
Said No L.E.A.P. Educator Ever

I have a deep, burning desire for my students to believe with all their hearts that no idea is too big or crazy. Why should anyone hinder the ideas we're passionately driven to pursue? The Wright brothers, Thomas Edison, JK Rowling, and Walt Disney are just a few of many innovators who felt inspired to persevere despite opposition and lack of support or funding.

* Wilbur and Orville Wright pursued their dream of flight without funding or even a college degree to support their venture.
* Thomas Edison became one of the greatest inventors ever known, even though his teachers told him he was "too stupid to learn anything."[2]
* JK Rowling's Harry Potter pitch was rejected by publishers twelve times.[3]
* Walt Disney was fired from the Kansas City Star because his editor felt he "lacked imagination and had no good ideas."[4]

Imagine if these individuals had given up in their pursuit to make their ideas become a reality. They had to fight discouragement from fears, doubts, and naysayers. Doing that required grit and tenacity—traits I believe our schools must strive to develop in students. Without question, our learners will face odds just as these great inventors did, but if we help them develop resiliency and encourage them to rely on their sense of curiosity, we can help ensure that they will follow their passions, use their creativity, and bravely take risks in the face of challenge.

Priming the Mind for Making

One of my favorite books is *What Do You Do with an Idea* by Kobi Yamada. Although it's a picture book, even our older students enjoy it and glean learning from its message. The story is about a child who discovers he has an idea and wonders where it came from. Afraid that others will think his idea is silly, the boy almost gives up on it and even attempts to ignore it. As the story progresses, the boy begins to nurture and feed his idea. Extraordinary change unfolds as his idea grows and evolves as a result of being nurtured.

During the read aloud, we take time to discuss what we see unfolding in the story and jot down our noticings about the character's behavior. We engage in vibrant discussions about the result of the boy nurturing his idea. Reading books like this one emphasizes risk-taking and resiliency and can be an excellent way to encourage learners to contemplate how they approach new situations or respond to adversity. You can even incorporate learning standards that encompass theme, character traits, cause and effect, and examine how the character evolves throughout the story. Independently, learners in my class generate lists or create webs of any and all ideas that they've ever had, big or small. After they've had the opportunity to brainstorm on their own, learners share their ideas with a partner then develop their ideas through the feedback or inquiries of others.

What's the Big Idea?

To inspire ideas to formulate, I often launch creative-thinking sessions by asking learners, "What would you make or create if you had all the materials and help that you required?" Encouraging them to consider what they enjoy doing versus dislike doing helps foster connections to what they would create by sparking new ideas. Depending on the age you work with or your focus, you may opt to narrow the question by being more specific; for example, you could

The Power of Independent Brainstorming

It's important to carve out time for learners to engage in independent brainstorming to get in touch with their individual thoughts rather than diving right into collaborative brainstorming. According to Keith Sawyer, author of *Group Genius,* "Decades of research have consistently shown that brainstorming groups think of far fewer ideas than the same number of people who work alone and later pool their ideas."[5] We need to support learners to connect and develop their own original thoughts prior to being influenced by others and avoid situations where one individual dominates the focus of the group. If groupthink takes form, students feel pressured to conform to the dominant view as opposed to sharing their unique or diverse ideas.[6] An added benefit of having learners brainstorm independently prior to engaging in a collaborative process is that when learners come together to share ideas, those who are less confident or quiet in nature have something prepared to contribute rather than feeling obligated to agree with the majority.

pose the question, "If you could add one item to our playground, what would it be?"

During independent and collaborative brainstorming sessions, I make my way around the room to talk with each student individually to check in on how they are doing. It's important to listen to the ideas of each individual and engage in conversation using reflective questioning. After this stage, learners reconvene with their partner and then in teams of four. Each time, I observe and listen to their interactions. In my experience, the more learners share ideas, the more their ideas seem to grow and blossom!

I fondly recall the time when one girl in my class expressed that she felt passionate about making music by forming a band. She explained that she never contemplated any kind of alternative because, in her mind, true band instruments were too expensive. It was at that point when the lightbulb went off! Her eyes widened, and she exclaimed with excitement, "Wait! I think we could find a way to make many different instruments and create our own small band!" Her enthusiasm was contagious. In time, she and her team created a variety of instruments and a small band that enjoyed composing new songs for our class. It's moments like this one that make me smile.

Sharing ideas may initially feel uncomfortable to some children or adults. Easing that discomfort starts by establishing a classroom culture where learners know they won't be judged for their ideas. From there, carving out independent brainstorming time as well as ample time to discuss ideas with a team will create the conditions to unleash incredible creative energy in your classroom. Even students who typically put up emotional walls to prevent others from seeing their academic struggles will gradually start to shine more brightly as they reveal their strengths.

When we demonstrate to kids that *we* believe they are makers and inventors, and that they have amazing ideas to contribute, something magical happens. Learners begin to carry themselves differently—more confidently. And, perhaps most importantly, they begin to grasp that through creative thinking, making, and exploration, they can design learning experiences for themselves rather than awaiting teacher direction.

Design Thinking Encourages and Deepens the Maker Mindset

Design Thinking can be used in all learning experiences and is not exclusive to maker education. It serves as an iterative method that promotes creative thinking by tapping into curiosities and fostering problem-solving skills. The five stages of Design Thinking can be easily modified to be applicable for all ages of learners.

* **Empathize or Understand:** Take time to understand the needs of whom you're designing for.
* **Define:** What is the problem? Ensure that questions are asked to clearly define the problem at hand.
* **Ideate:** Get all ideas out by writing them down, then discussing. Sketch designs and label all aspects.
* **Prototype:** Create the design and make adjustments during the creation stage if necessary.
* **Test:** See if your product or design serves as a solution to the original problem and meets the needs of whom you're designing for.

DESIGN THINKING

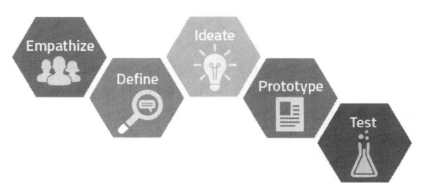

I want to note that Design Thinking doesn't always have to happen in the exact order stated. There may be times that you start at different stages depending on what you're doing. Incorporating Design Thinking supports learners in identifying a purpose for what they're making or exploring. Whether it's summarizing a story on video, creating a musical instrument, exploring natural phenomenon, or coding robotics, the design cycle supports meaningful learning. We also use it within problem- and project-based learning as well as STEAM. In maker education, play or tinkering is a component not to be ignored, as children of all ages learn through free exploration, too. By embedding Design Thinking, we support learners to be more metacognitive about what they're creating, why they're creating it, and how they can improve their work. It also provides a system for thinking, and through it, learners grow into problem-solvers, divergent thinkers, and purposeful explorers.

Launching Makerspace

Are you ready to take the L.E.A.P. and incorporate innovative learning opportunities for students? Educator Laura Fleming, author of *Worlds of Making* and *The Kickstart Guide to Making Great Makerspaces* shared a tip for transforming learning with me:

> I provide my students with the access to the tools, materials, supplies, and space they need to be innovative, but, ultimately, the opportunities come from within themselves. My role as an educator is to work hard to create the conditions for them to want to make and innovate, as opposed to forcing them to do those things. It is so much more authentic when done in this way, and the things they do accomplish as a result endure with them—well beyond the school day, or even upon graduation.

Many teachers have incorporated writing and literacy into maker education and tied it to the curriculum. If you're feeling that you're uncertain how to create time for maker education, consider how you can integrate it into learning. Making shouldn't be relegated to the makerspace; in fact, it can have an even have greater impact when it's woven into content for authentic learning.

Questions to Support and Guide the Process of Integrating Maker Education

Because each makerspace is best when personalized to the unique needs and interests of learners and their school community, I hope you'll ask the following questions when taking the L.E.A.P. to launch a makerspace.

* What is your vision of makerspace for student learning opportunities?
* What are your desired student outcomes and learning goals?
* Taking student voice into account, what materials, resources, and opportunities are desired?
* How can you differentiate as well as personalize learning opportunities?
* Will the makerspace be a dedicated location, organized on carts to be signed out, or a component that's accessible within every classroom for natural integration of making throughout the school day?
* How can you lead the charge for maker education with teachers and students to ensure everyone understands the benefits and feels supported in integrating it in learning experiences?

Next Steps

* Create a wish list of donations to be sent home to families.
* Share the wish list with local businesses and foster partnerships; they're a win-win because donations are tax write-offs for businesses.
* Develop a system to efficiently organize donations as they come in.
* Visit local stores to request items that are typically tossed aside (e.g., cardboard boxes, shipping and packing materials).
* Seek grant opportunities to support learners as well.
* Involve local experts who can lead how-to classes based on student interest or provide feedback and tips to projects created by learners using Design Thinking.
* Routinely meet with learners, educators, and community stakeholders to empower all voices. That will ensure the most dynamic opportunities are made available.

L.E.A.P. Onward

When we lay the foundation of a luminous culture through relationships and empowered learning and then enhance it through the development of critical thinking, problem-solving, empathy, and understanding, learners begin to assimilate how to manage themselves by being more reflective. This kind of classroom culture lessens the likelihood of chaos. Trust me when I say that behavior management charts and point systems become irrelevant. As a result of cultivating a maker culture, instruction time is more efficient and meaningful as learners engage in the design-thinking process and develop genuine ownership over their learning. Literature crafted to support the development of creative risk-taking helps learners understand that there are endless possibilities for learning when it comes to our imagination and ideas. This understanding primes the brain through iterative design.

Fleming notes, "Don't be afraid to give up control and to allow the opportunities for students to take control of their own learning. If I would have limited my students to the things that are within my comfort zone and within my scope of knowledge, they would never have accomplished so many of the amazing things that they have done." *Embracing a maker culture encourages learners to evolve as creative risk-takers and innovators.*

L.E.A.P. Tips and Takeaways

* Integrate literature that incorporates learning standards and concepts connected to cultivating the maker mindset.
* Provide opportunities for learners to contemplate their big ideas and share with peers.
* Infuse Design Thinking to encourage a deeper understanding and application of learning.
* Empower voices of learners by involving them in the development of maker education.
* Create maker education opportunities that are unique to your school community; don't look to duplicate another school, as needs often vary.
* Have students create their own inventions based on a need or problem to be solved. Even creating a prototype allows for the divergent thinking and maker-mindset to develop.

L.E.A.P. beyond Your Boundaries

Share your reflections, questions, and ideas using #LEAPeffect.

1. What topics do you teach in the curriculum that could be enhanced through maker education?
2. Within your school week or day, where could you carve out time to provide learners with opportunities to make or create based on their passions and interests?

Chapter 10
Passion-Infused Learning

Passion is one great force that unleashes
creativity, because if you're passionate about
something, then you're more willing to take risks.

—Yo-Yo Ma

Have you ever felt so alive and inspired while working on something that you couldn't bring yourself to stop? Or perhaps you have an idea that you have returned to time and time again to explore in your mind. Our passions, combined with curiosity, have a way of drawing us into learning and discovery like nothing else. As educators, our job is to cocreate experiences with our learners to evoke that kind of passion for learning.

When I was with my students one afternoon, we began discussing what they enjoy and dislike in general about school throughout the years. Typically, I use student surveys, but this was more of a casual class conversation late in the spring, as our culture supported risk-taking, and learners also had the choice to share or not. Sharing what they enjoy was simple. Their responses included, "I like that we get to choose how to show what we're learning because we can be as creative as we want" and "We get to explore and take time to create work that we actually care about!"

The response that hit me most powerfully came from Ella, who said, "This year, our ideas and what we're interested in learning matters. You respect who we are and have helped us develop passions." Coming from a nine-year-old, and voiced so articulately, Ella's statement opened my eyes to why infusing learners' passions is so critical. What I have learned is that personal interests can inspire curiosity, draw in learners, and spark intrinsic motivation. But empowering learners by leveraging their strengths and passions communicates to them that who they are as unique individuals matters. It also demonstrates that school doesn't have to be limited to what *we* want or have to teach students, but that the focus should always be on the learner.

It was enlightening (and encouraging) to hear the positive comments shared by my students about learning, but I knew I needed to be vulnerable enough to ask what they didn't enjoy about school. It's human nature to want to avoid answers to questions that may make us uncomfortable, but it provides so much insight to reflect best. Classically speaking, it's taboo for students to tell a teacher what they dislike; some educators may even view those student opinions as disrespectful. But student voice matters! If we aren't asking what they like and *don't like,* we can't provide truly relevant learning experiences.

Todd, who was new to our school, piped up and said, "All throughout my past school years, most days I just came to school, sat down to morning work, followed directions, and completed classwork throughout the school day, then did homework after school. Teachers sometimes added in games or had us collaborate with others, but I can't remember a time when we got to choose how to show our learning or ever work on projects of our choice. I just thought learning and school were about memorizing and then taking tests to show what I know." He continued, "What I would like is to learn more through project-based learning because that's when I feel I like learning the most." Todd's input provided insight on how he had viewed school and learning itself.

You and I both know that memorization and test taking do not lead to authentic learning. Most likely, Todd's teachers didn't believe those things were the sum of education either. But, like so many educators do, they got stuck in a rut. Perhaps they felt unsupported or unsure of how to innovate. Regardless of the reasons it exists, an uninspired learning environment has unintended and adverse effects on learners. From Todd, I realized that I needed to do more with project-based learning than I already was, or seek ways to infuse elements of it in all areas of teaching and learning.

Asking for my students' input and perspective has helped me to understand how students perceive learning in school. In the past, for example, some students expressed that they disliked our ELA routines that were scripted through our mandated programs. In all transparency, many of my colleagues and I shared the same feelings as our students. Although we were required to follow it with fidelity, we tried to identify ways to integrate various protocols and weave in our own creative touches to engage learners and create relevancy. Still, the lessons lacked the depth we envisioned. Fortunately, over the course of time, our voices, combined with those of our students, were heard by our administration, who gave us the green light to innovate the structure of our ELA program. We used the mandates as a guide and resource rather than a script.

If you are in a school or district where you see areas for improvement or have ideas for creating greater student engagement and empowerment, share your ideas for authentic learning with your administration. It may require repetition and persistence. It may even require that you share your students' voices as well, so be sure that you ask for their input! If your goal, like mine, is to create the best possible learning experiences for your students, do what you can as you innovate inside the system even as you continue to seek the support of those in school and district leadership for greater changes.

Not every single thing we do in school will incorporate the passions of learners, but the goal should be to tap into those passions as often as possible. That starts with understanding their likes and dislikes. I noted our class discussion earlier in the chapter, but surveys are another way to gather insights from learners. What you learn will help you identify ways to empower students to create authentic learning experiences. Here are a few questions you can ask. (Note that questions should vary based on the time of year.)

1. What have you enjoyed so far about this year?
2. What are your favorite ways to learn?
3. What are your favorite activities/projects/etc. (even from past years) and why?
4. What do you enjoy learning about?
5. If you could change something about this year, what would it be?
6. How could I make learning even more interesting for next year's students?

Infusing Passions

Infusing passions can be the game-changer that fosters robust, authentic learning and intrinsic motivation. As we've discussed, learners first need to have some idea about what interests them. Uncovering their strengths and exposing students to a variety of topics and experiences is a great place to start the process of helping them find their passions. Another way to dig deeper into this process is to have learners independently create lists and engage in whole-class and small-group discussions about one or more of the following questions:

* What do you want learning to be like in school?
* What are you most curious about?
* If you had the option to learn about anything, what would you choose?
* What concerns you in our world or influences you to want to create a solution to the problem?
* What impact do you hope to have on others?

Learning Through the Eyes of Students

Every classroom may take a different approach to infusing passions; the purpose of the list of questions above is to provide a handful of suggestions to get the conversation started. You can get things rolling by sharing some of the possibilities of what school could look like. Sometimes an example from you can provoke students to think beyond what they know about and have experienced in schools. When learners engage in possibility thinking, the ideas flow as they share what they would like for learning to be—based on their interests and what excites them.

To help spark their imagination, I may ask, "Who enjoys creating videocasts, cartooning, creating skits, podcasting, creating books, or writing?" Work with learners to help them choose how to demonstrate their learning, and then share with an audience to bring authenticity to their work. Within any content or learning experience, learners can create any one of the ideas listed above as examples, or even a combination to capture their learning in a documentary fashion and summarize their understandings. This is one of the most basic ways to begin incorporating passions into education and fostering the conditions for student ownership. In Chapter 12, we will explore this more closely as we identify ways to share learning with an authentic audience. By integrating passions into what you're currently doing, you give students greater autonomy over their learning, and this serves as the foundation to support student-led inquiry and passion projects.

Curiosity Sparks Motivation

Educators spend a great deal of time talking about engagement and empowerment strategies, and these are undoubtedly important to leverage, but curiosity is another critical and often overlooked component of learning. Research suggests that when individuals are curious about a topic, memory improves.[1] One study found that a "curious personality was linked to a wide range of adaptive behaviors, including tolerance of anxiety and uncertainty, positive emotional expressiveness, initiation of humor and playfulness, unconventional thinking, and a non-defensive, and a non-critical attitude."[2] These adaptive behaviors are essential to fostering a culture of innovation and even contribute to the development of a growth mindset.

Infusing passions based on wonderings is one way to spark curiosity in learning. Sometimes, however, learners struggle to identify something that inspires them to feel curious. As a society, we all move so fast and rely so heavily on instant information that we rarely take time to slow down, engage in mindfulness, and say, "I'm curious about . . ."

Give your students (And yourself!) time to ponder. Write "I wonder" statements together. Ask questions that challenge learners to identify their curiosities, such as "I wonder . . . what does the inside of a computer look like?" or "I wonder . . . how authors decide on a topic to write about." Identifying curiosities may start while exploring a topic in school, which is why maintaining a notebook of interests and questions is a great way for learners to develop greater awareness to support them in infusing passions in their learning.

Personal Interests Catapult Agency

In Chapter 3, I shared about Marie, my student who tested every possible boundary. She lacked motivation in a way that I had never experienced with a child. Attempting to get her to comply only made her push further away. Knowing that I needed to support the growth of the whole child, I had to employ patience and figure out what was going to motivate her to want to do something—*anything*. With social and emotional support at the heart of my mission, I struggled to successfully motivate her when she appeared apathetic in class. Other times, it was a challenge to help navigate her learning when she exhibited oppositional behaviors. Little by little, with a focus on cultivating an authentic relationship and creating the conditions that fostered agency, she started to blossom. Allowing her to pursue her interest in art as part of her learning allowed her to have the control she required and, in turn, engagement began to soar.

Before long, she was creating animated cartoons using an app that offered learners the ability to personalize characters and integrate voiceover narration. Marie leveraged this app to explain math problems creatively. In ELA, she was empowered to draw and animate illustrations that captured how a particular character changed from the beginning to the end of the story. When we launched passion projects, she immediately knew what she was going to explore and avidly took on the project of learning about what it would take for her to become a professional cartoonist. Yes, she *still* had her moments and required a lot of social-emotional support; however, little shifts led to the desired change.

In an interview with Daniel Pink, he explained that "If we really want engagement rather than compliance, we have to increase the degree of autonomy that people have over what they do; over how, when, and where they do it; and over whom they do it with."[3] In Marie's case, compliance was never going to be an option as she vied for control. But we were able to foster engagement, which triggered empowerment through autonomy over how to learn and communicate her thinking.

When we have some degree of independence over how and what we do, we naturally feel motivated. For our students, autonomy can shift learning from something they *have* to do to something they *want* to do. From learners who are defiant to those who are painfully quiet and reserved, all students benefit from agency that empowers them to use their voice and choice to explore personal interests as part of their learning experience.

What Matters Compels Action

It's profoundly moving to witness a child feel compelled to take action as an agent of change. Sure, we can tell kids to volunteer, but it's powerful to see a child or young adult take charge and work to make a difference in the world. In episode thirteen of the LeadUpTeach podcast, Don Wettrick shared an example of a learner who tackled social entrepreneurship. A young lady in his high school innovation class made the connection that people in poverty tend to eat unhealthily and that, ironically, those same people who have less food to eat tend to suffer from obesity. After researching the topic, she learned about the Fair Food Network's Double Up Bucks program in Detroit. As stated on their website, "The Double Up Bucks program doubles the value of federal nutrition (SNAP or food stamps) benefits spent at participating markets and grocery stores, helping people bring home more healthy fruits and vegetables while supporting local farmers. The wins are three-fold: low-income consumers eat more healthy food, local farmers gain new customers and make more money, and more food dollars stay in the local economy."[4]

Wettrick's student realized she could bring the change to her community. She felt concern over the fact that people in poverty have less access to fresh fruits and vegetables. She also realized that if she could create a solution to help people in poverty, a secondary benefit was that it would support her local economy. After going to the farmers' market to discuss this matter with those in charge, they decided that if she could assist, they were interested. Wettrick's student used school resources to make her vision a reality. Using a laser engraver and balsa wood, she designed her own coin and design layout as a token for individuals to use at the farmers' market to purchase food. Meanwhile, she worked alongside the food stamp coordinator of the county to ensure a portion of individuals' food stamps could be credited for the market. The result of her effort was that she helped people on food stamps begin eating more healthfully, spurred the local economy, and raised awareness for the farmers' market. This student also went on to be the food stamp coordinator for the farmers' market. Wettrick reflects that not everything went well for this student, as she hit many walls along the way. But what's important is that she persisted, identified whom to talk to, and which direction to go next.

We need our learners to determine what truly matters to them because when something matters, they feel concern and a sense of urgency to take action and make a change. After all, the pinnacle of learning is having a positive impact on someone, or even society as a whole, as did Edison and Einstein. Everything about what this student did models real life, and she was able to explore it all within her innovation class that is reflective of Genius Hour. We need to get to the heart of what profoundly matters to our kids by helping them identify problems that exist in our school, community, or world.

Encouraging the L.E.A.P.

As an innovator or early adopter himself, Wettrick also shared with us how other change agents can best navigate through resistance or even skepticism when incorporating variations of innovation time or genius hour to infuse passion into learning. His advice is to "get people on your team. Ask for help and involve other educators within your school to help you make it happen. When everyone is involved, there's not an outlier that experiences isolation."[5]

In a conversation I had with Joy Kirr, author of *Shift This!,* she offered very similar advice. Reflecting on her own experiences of isolation, Kirr told me she learned the importance of approaching colleagues and sharing ideas then seeking to employ their help. Educators naturally want to help, and we all want to feel valued by our colleagues and acknowledged as a difference-maker for kids. If we always take steps forward and innovate in isolation, we'll continue to be alone. Reach out. Share your resources and ideas, and ask for help to encourage others to develop a shared ownership of the vision and embark on the journey with you. And, as Kirr states, "You don't have to dive in all at once to make huge, positive change."[6] Following this approach, we can stretch the metaphoric rubber band to grow beyond our zone of comfort and encourage our colleagues to do the same.

L.E.A.P. Onward

How you choose to integrate passion-infused learning is ultimately up to you and what works best for your learners. It's easy to get caught up thinking that there's only one right way to do this. The temptation may be to believe that it can only be done through genius hour or passion projects. But as Kirr explained in our conversation, it's helpful to start slowly by getting to know learners and helping them to understand what matters most to them. Laying that groundwork develops the foundation for learners to understand what their passions are. Connect with educators and take time to learn more while also being transparent about what you're trying in your own classroom. As an innovator yourself, consider how you can launch passion-infused learning to be authentic with your students. Each year, learning may look different as you reflect and retool methods to meet your learners' needs. Use the Design Thinking model to develop your own variation of passion-infused learning.

L.E.A.P. Tips and Takeaways

* Take time to learn students' interests.
* Infuse choice on a daily basis by allowing learners to select how to demonstrate their learning.
* Help learners start to identify how they'd like learning to look and feel.
* Engage in activities that spark curiosity and carve out time for learners to consider what they wonder about or are interested in learning.
* Expose learners to problems in our world and support them as problem seekers to help them identify what genuinely matters to them.

* Have learners designate a notebook as their passion or idea journal to keep track of their thoughts or maintain a blog where they can receive feedback from peers as well as connect with others who share similar passions to grow them more fully.
* Collect perceptual data from students at the middle and/or end of the year to prove that this is a valuable use of time.

L.E.A.P. beyond Your Boundaries

Share your reflections, questions, and ideas using #LEAPeffect.

1. In what areas do learners currently have choice in learning?
2. Thinking of your current schedule and how you structure learning, how can you infuse students' passions to a greater extent?
3. Within your school week or day, where could you carve out time to provide learners with opportunities to explore their passions?

Chapter 11
The Power of Project-Based Learning

We need students who can learn how
to learn, who can discover how to push
themselves and are generous enough and
honest enough to engage with the outside
world to make those dreams happen.

—Seth Godin

Listening to learners buzz with excitement as they create driving questions and immerse themselves in a project that authentically incorporates their strengths and interests thrills me as an educator! Grateful for the opportunity to experience professional learning on project-based learning (PBL) straight from the Buck Institute for Education (BIE) on multiple occasions, I continue to grow in my understanding as I learn alongside students and my team. As with anything else, PBL can be modified to suit the needs of each learner. We can innovate and iterate within a broad structure of PBL. Although this chapter provides an understanding of the foundation of PBL to incorporate elements into your classroom, I highly recommend reading about project-based learning or engaging in professional learning to gain a deeper understanding and then making the necessary adjustments to suit your learners.

My deep appreciation for PBL comes from the opportunities it provides students, including authentic learning, voice and choice, future-ready skill development, and agency. By engaging learners in PBL, we create the conditions for learners to develop their own learning experiences. Project-based learning can often be misinterpreted as a project, but the two are distinctly different, as noted in the chart on the next page.

Projects may have their place in education, but to create a culture of innovation, we must employ flexible structures that empower agency and real-world learning. As we take a look at the elements of PBL, we'll explore how they can be infused within any classroom. Since this is not an in-depth guide on how to facilitate learning through PBL, I highly recommend visiting BIE.org and reading *Hacking Project Based Learning* by Ross Cooper and Erin Murphy to take a deeper dive. Both have been instrumental in my implementation of PBL.

PBL units are known for incorporating an authentic, overarching topic that evokes curiosity or a sense of urgency. PBL allows learners to explore their passion and take action; it empowers them to incite change that solves a real problem. Overlapping commonalities of infusing passions and maker education are embedded throughout PBL. Let's take a look at an example of this.

Differences between a Project
and Project-Based Learning

Project	Project-Based Learning
Direction based	Inquiry based
Teacher creates the directions, steps, and the end goal	Is open-ended: learners create driving questions, what they need to know, and how to share their work and with whom
Vague connection to students' passions and strengths	Obvious connection to students' passions and strengths
Often created to summarize learning, and not typically connected to a real-world solution or authentic call to action	May provide real-world solutions or call to action
Model, diorama, illustration, or poster	May include a proposal to suggest change and a detailed plan for the steps they will take
Outcome based	Impact based

Our fourth-grade team constructed a PBL unit on The Human Footprint that focused on learning standards, including informational writing based on evidence from a variety of texts and media. While this unit is rich with numerous ELA standards, we had priority standards that drove our planning.

We started with a twofold approach to consider 1) what our learners need to learn, and 2) what was going to motivate them to feel that they are part of the solution to the problem of pollution in a way that made learning compelling.

It was important for our team to ensure that we weren't just blindly diving into a project without learning objectives and success skills tied to it. Nor did we want this to feel teacher-driven. The goal was to raise awareness of The Human Footprint and identify unique solutions as part of a call to action. We wanted learners to feel empowered as environmental scientists. They would also need to acquire research and essential writing skills through the experience. Even though we created the structure, we intentionally left room for student ownership. From there, we worked backward. Even with the framework for success we created, we had to retool the framework in the process.

Ideally, in PBL, the best topics are chosen based on a question or problem brought up in class that sparked curiosity and conversation, in a similar manner to the STEAM and NASA example mentioned in Chapter 5, under connectedness. But in some cases, we may be required to teach a topic within the curriculum and then seek ways to incorporate it within PBL creatively. In our situation, we were participating in summer professional learning and planning our PBL prior to the school year with the BIE's support. We had always taught about The Human Footprint and decided to renovate how we previously facilitated learning by teaching the concept through PBL. There are numerous variations of PBL, and we can leverage powerful elements

What We Planned vs. What We Left Open

Here's what we knew in advance to launching our project:

- How we would launch the project to provoke curiosity
- The role our students would take on
- Which resources we would use initially to stimulate learning
- Initial expert connections to scaffold learning and foster an authentic experience
- The instructional strategies that we would embed
- The reflection protocols that would be infused
- How students would engage in critique and revision and which protocols we'd use
- Our timeframe
- Students would write an informational piece using evidence from a variety of sources

We created opportunities for ...

- Students to create driving questions
- Students to leverage their strengths and passions
- Students to select which experts to connect with
- How students would share their learning with an authentic audience
- The creation of mini-lessons to target the specific needs of students
- How students would curate their learning and present their project
- Possibilities for students to take action through service learning and become advocates

to enhance learning. Our goal here is to embed the elements of PBL leading to skill development and the fostering of curiosity, divergent thinking, and wonder in students. Learning begins to unfold naturally within PBL.

The 7 Elements of PBL

Using the project our team created, we'll take a close look at how our teacher team embedded the seven elements of PBL and infused learners' passions in this unit. Keep in mind that the elements that follow are applicable for all grade levels. The content, priority standards, student interactions, and level of support will vary depending on the developmental stage of your learners. With that said, when we create a culture that empowers learning and provide the appropriate level of structure and agency, students will rise to the occasion.

1. Authenticity

What problems exist that are relevant to your learners or their future? Some issues that may seem insignificant to adults are important to learners or *would be* important to them following exposure.

In our case, my team and I knew that students from previous years didn't know what to recycle versus what to toss into the garbage. We could have told them what to do or directed their attention to the graphic that hung on the wall that explicitly indicated what items were to get recycled or tossed. But telling or even showing students what to do doesn't lead to deep learning. Comprehending the *why* behind a behavior or directive drives home understanding, so we wanted to immerse learners in experiences that helped them to grasp the detriment of pollution. Before our PBL, the topic of pollution, or how it affects every living creature and the planet, had no relevance to our students. In their eyes, it wasn't an authentic problem—yet.

2. Launching a Project

The project launch is one of the most essential elements to consider. I equate it to a first impression. Instead of standing in front of your class and announcing that learners are going to explore the effects of pollution, think of ways in which you could creatively spark their curiosity.

As a team, we brainstormed ideas that would both expose students to the issues and pique their interests. Some of those ideas included the following:

* We could have a naturalist visit our students from a nearby nature center with a couple of animals in tow. The expert guest would explain the detrimental effects of pollution on the critters in their care and elicit the students' help in bringing awareness to the community.
* We could show thought-provoking videos from National Geographic that demonstrated the amount of resources used to create items such as milk jugs and diapers and how manufacturing those things affects the earth.
* We could invite in an environmental scientist who could lead a hands-on learning experience to foster awareness in our learners and spark curiosity to encourage inquiry.

Ultimately, we wanted learners to feel as if they were contributing a meaningful solution to an issue that was bigger than themselves or even our school community. As we watched their understanding unfold, we saw that our learners became invested in the mission of their work. We knew that for experience be relevant to them, we had to tug on their hearts and help them to grasp the depth of problems that exist as a result of pollution.

As you plan ways to kick off a PBL experience, consider inviting in experts or engaging learners through dynamic and unforgettable happenings. Your launch could include showing a video that captures your learners' attention and stirs wonder and awe. A room transformation is another way to set the stage for authentic learning. (I recently read about a teacher who chose to cover the classroom with litter. Upon returning to the classroom, learners were shocked by the room's appearance.) Setting the stage creates a connection for learners.

One highly engaging project launch example occurred when my husband, Michael Bostwick, who serves as an intermediate school principal, elicited shock and awe for the ultimate hook. A team of teachers were launching a project to improve a local zoo, so he ran through the hallways with a cage in search of an escaped animal. Students watched his antics, somewhat bewildered, just before walking into their classroom; once inside, they were greeted by a trailer about endangered animals, which preceded a visit from a zookeeper who had brought animals with her. Immense excitement ensued and learners were clearly riveted.

However you opt to launch learning, tailor it to your learners' interests and what will pique curiosity.

3. Develop Driving Questions

Once learners realize the depth of the problem related to their project and curiosity is sparked, they begin to formulate their own questions around the driving question posed by the teacher. In our project, the driving question was the following: "How can you, as an environmentalist, propose a project to reduce your community's human footprint?"

Ask learners what they wonder about in relation to the chosen topic following the launch. What more do they want or need to know? Have them brainstorm as many questions as they possibly can. Remember that it's best to first have learners brainstorm a list of questions independently and then share and discuss with a partner or in small teams. From there, come together as a whole group and share out, preventing groupthink. If this is a new practice for your class, it may start off slowly, but it gains traction the more their peers pose questions. Keep in mind that some questions will seem to have obvious answers, and sometimes kids will ask questions that are unrelated to the topic. That's okay! Asking questions promotes divergent thinking, so be intentional about not rejecting questions; instead, redirect them to an idea journal.

As learners share their questions, I type them so that they can be projected and viewed on our whiteboard. Before long, we have a lengthy list compiled of all that they wonder. There's immense power behind learners *asking* questions rather than simply responding to them with an answer.

After drafting questions, we next explore how to identify open versus closed questions through discussion. The intent is to avoid (or limit) questions that can be answered with an internet search; far deeper thinking is needed to develop open-ended questions that require further research.

Closed question: What causes land pollution?

Open question: What products are already created to help The Human Footprint, and how can we improve their functionality or design to make a greater impact?

As a group, we eliminate the closed questions and are then left with a selection that are more open ended and promote inquiry. At this point, learners write on a sticky note the question that intrigues and elicits passion in them. This becomes their driving question. Afterward, students are teamed up based on their driving questions and the type of pollution that makes them most curious. It's okay if their questions vary slightly, they'll either choose to select one and work collaboratively on it or maintain their own question but still support one another. I've seen success with both options. Students move along the agency spectrum past engagement into empowerment when that choice is given.

4. Inquiry

Inquiry triggers curiosity related to a question, scenario, or problem. The objective is to stimulate thinking and inspire students to drive their learning and uncover solutions or answers through research and conversations. BIE defines inquiry as the following:

> In PBL, inquiry is iterative; when confronted with a challenging problem or question, students ask questions, find resources to help answer them, then ask deeper questions—and the process repeats until a satisfactory solution or answer is developed. Projects can incorporate different information sources, mixing the traditional idea of "research"—reading a book or searching a website—with more real-world, field-based interviews with experts, service providers, and users. Students also might inquire into the needs of the users of a product they're creating in a project, or the audience for a piece of writing or multimedia.[1]

It's easy to "cover" content, but engaging learners through inquiry can motivate them to ask and seek answers to their own questions. Inquiry can be incorporated into any area of learning and elicits both divergent and critical-thinking skills.

5. Reflection for All

In Chapter 6, we explored the importance of reflection in connection with empowering learning. Deep reflection is critical within all areas of learning and promotes growth.

While our students engage in reflection frequently throughout PBL, we as educators reflect deeply just as often. Reflecting on our project, we felt excited about our plan and launch. Initially we found our resources to fit but changed them as we discovered new or better texts or videos. Much of our reflection took place as we moved forward day by day with the project. It was essential that we reflected on our plan, the response from learners, and feedback from expert partnerships. From our reflection, we were able to retool daily and identify what worked well and what we needed to change. Also, reflecting with one another served as a support system, too. On several occasions we were uncertain if what we were doing was the best approach, and hearing each other's insights, tips, and strategies was invaluable! We also took ample time to comb through formative assessments to decide how to best support learners through mini-lessons that were personalized to small groups of students.

In all transparency, during our first year of implementing PBL, we felt most confident with the teacher-planned sections, as opposed to the stage where learners begin to take ownership over the direction of their project. I vividly recall the feeling of uncertainty that set in once the teacher-planned sections had been completed. We suddenly realized that it was time to turn learners loose, and we didn't know exactly what that would look like. We shifted from serving as the facilitators of learning to supporters. The diverse groups were all working under the same umbrella of The Human Footprint, but each had unique pathways associated with their individual driving questions. We had to reflect on our learning and loosely plan for what resources our learners may require in the days to come. Rather than planning explicit teaching of content, we found ourselves taking more time to identify how we could better structure collaborative feedback as well as critique and revision protocols. In the end, our learners demonstrated greater agency over learning, and engagement skyrocketed!

6. Critique and Revision

In my geeky love of education, I have to admit that critique and revision is one of my favorite aspects of PBL. Similar to Design Thinking, where individuals share a prototype and test or seek feedback within critique and revision, learners share their project ideas and then receive feedback in order to retool their project based on the input from others. As with any feedback protocol, it's essential to ensure the culture supports learners to feel safe sharing their ideas and questions. Additionally, keep in mind that receiving feedback from peers can feel intimidating to some. Creating structures that promote rich, useful feedback supports the process.

To help students learn how to provide effective feedback, start by asking for input on something that isn't connected to an individual and guide learners through the process; for example, you could use a picture drawn by someone they don't know, or even the structure of lunch in the cafeteria or recess, to develop a broad understanding. Set targets for the feedback to ensure everyone has a focus, and explicitly state that feedback should be *helpful*, *kind*, and *specific* to the target. Feedback isn't about opinions. To maintain a luminous culture, learners have to be cognizant of facial expressions or comments that may cause their peers to shrink back. Feedback through critique and revision can be extremely effective when the culture supports it and learners understand how to frame their thoughts. This is especially true when it's done daily as part of the framework of instruction and learning.

Help learners to frame feedback by making it positive and supportive to encourage the improvement of their peers. Some suggestions based on our professional learning through BIE and what's proven to be successful in the classroom include the following:

* **Use of "I" statements:** I wonder . . . I found the chart to be helpful . . . I'm not understanding what you mean, could you reword?
* **Pose Questions:** I'm curious why you didn't include an illustration. Why did you choose to interview one particular expert rather than two or three in the field? How might you design . . . ?
* **State Positives Before Providing a Suggestion:** I really like how you designed your action plan, but wonder if you can actually do follow through with it as-is.

After practicing giving feedback through modeling and coaching, determine if learners require more practice prior to the actual process of critiquing leading to revision.

One protocol that has been effective for critique and revision for our learners is a gallery walk done silently to allow learners to think independently and really consider the work of their peers. Individuals or teams of learners first organize their project plan by neatly listing their driving question, how they will acquire their learning or information, who their target audience is, what experts will be interviewed, and their action plan to make a difference or raise awareness on large chart paper. The chart paper is posted around the room for students to review.

To not sway the thoughts and feedback of others, learners write their feedback on the sticky side of a sticky note and then, on the front, place a plus sign on the positive feedback and a delta to specify feedback for possible revisions. This strategy is highly effective in all content areas; we utilize it frequently during math to encourage learners to analyze how their peers problem-solved.

The gallery walk is just one of many protocols you can use to support learners through the critique and revision process. The goal with using multiple protocols is to embed the practices of critique and revision so that they become routine. I encourage the use of Socratic seminar (for feedback and discussion) often. This encourages students to remain engaged and empowered by acknowledging their thoughts with evidence as well as trying to persuade/challenge others' thinking.

Student Project Gallery Walk Protocol
Setup and Directions   • Hang poster or arrange projects for the gallery walk.   • Distribute sticky notes.   • Assign roles (give students specific elements of the project to critique).   • Provide directions.
Gallery Walk & Feedback   • Silently record feedback on sticky notes, specific "I likes" and "I wonders."   • Give one "I like" and one "I wonder" for each project.   • Make sure the feedback is helpful, specific, and kind.
Reflection   • Think deeply about your project using the feedback received by your peers and how you can use it to strengthen your work.

After critique protocols, learners review their feedback forms to consider revision. As the facilitators of learning, we may need to help reframe thoughts to be even more specific or support learners through coaching to help them best compose useful feedback. All in all, this process models real-world critique and revision, and learners become more thoughtful in their work by reflecting on their peers' work and their own.

7. Authentic Audience

An authentic audience brings purpose to the work that learners engage in. Instead of handing in a final product for a grade, learners connect with stakeholders who connect to the topic of their project to make their action plan come full circle with the hopes of having a positive impact on society. In Chapter 12, we are going to bring it all together by taking a deeper dive into sharing with an authentic audience. We will explore the possibilities and how we can infuse it into many areas of learning.

L.E.A.P. Onward

Learners will undoubtedly reap the benefits of engaging in PBL. Incorporating the seven elements of PBL into learning brings authenticity to the classroom. Students are encouraged to see that education isn't simply about mastering the content but about developing the essential success skills to deepen and improve learning. Furthermore, if we empower learners to create a call to action and make their work service- or entrepreneurship-oriented, they develop pathways that elevate their experiences and practice skills essential for future success. We need to support learners to connect the dots to understand why school is relevant to their life, and PBL is one avenue to do just that. Ultimately, our goal is to create future leaders who will keep our country globally competitive.

L.E.A.P. Tips and Takeaways

* Identify topics that are relevant or would be relevant to your learners following exposure.
* Launch learning in creative manners using video, setting the stage, bringing in community members, or through other efforts to capture learners' attention.
* Leverage the power of inquiry and learner-created questions, particularly open questions that promote deep thinking, wonder, and curiosity.
* Incorporate protocols for critique and revision. These protocols can be utilized in every area and foster a culture of feedback and retooling based on reflection.
* Create opportunities for learners to take action within their community. Doing so has a direct impact on the community and, in turn, naturally fuels the drive for students to continue learning on their own.

L.E.A.P. beyond Your Boundaries

Share your reflections, questions, and ideas using #LEAPeffect.

1. How could you incorporate various elements of project-based learning in your daily practice?
2. Consider a unit within the curriculum that you teach. In what ways could you reshape it to include the elements of project-based learning?

Part IV
Potential Soars

Chapter 12
Bringing It Together

The world needs dreamers and the world
needs doers. But above all what the world
needs most are dreamers that do.

—Sarah Ban Breathnach

In *The Element: How Finding Your Passion Changes Everything*, Ken Robinson writes, "The fact is that given the challenges we face, education doesn't need to be reformed—it needs to be transformed. The key to this transformation is not to standardize education, but to personalize it, to build achievement on discovering the individual talents of each child, to put students in an environment where they want to learn and where they can naturally discover their true passions."[1] As educators, we're constantly innovating as we rethink and retool the learning opportunities and experiences we bring to students. In our effort to transform a system developed in the industrial era, we've identified avenues that support us in our journey. Our world today requires makers, creators, and service-oriented individuals who embrace future success skills and entrepreneurial thinking.

By invoking passion, we support learners to recognize what inspires them to learn more and, as a result, to take action.

Cultivating the maker mindset, infusing passions, and embedding elements of project-based learning not only increase engagement and empowered learning but also have the potential to develop skills that are essential for life beyond school. As mentioned in the introduction, this section is not a manual or rigid recipe to improve learning for kids; it does, however, contain the ingredients vital for mixing up the dynamic experiences for your unique learners. Creating authentic learning demands that we use these components on a regular basis.

Without question, it would be time-consuming to implement maker education, passion projects, *and* project-based learning as separate entities in our classrooms. That's why I advocate for infusing the overlapping components of each of these teaching methods to create the most relevant learning opportunities for students. Choice, opportunities to leverage technology as a tool, personal goal setting, and reflection, as well as the 6Cs of reimagining learning (curiosity, creativity, communication, critical thinking, collaboration, and connectedness) are evident in maker education, passion projects, and project-based learning. As discussed, these kinds of learning experiences should be as accessible as possible, not kept in silos. They should be incorporated into *all* content areas. By using the components of maker education, passion-infused learning, and PBL, we create gateways for learners to identify their true passions, which will motivate them to be action oriented. Launching mini-projects that encapsulate the content you're teaching and infuse the components of authentic learning is a great way to begin.

> **The first step is to establish that something**
> **is possible; then probability will occur.**
>
> **—Elon Musk**

An Authentic Audience Creates Meaningful Learning

Bringing together learning experiences by sharing with an authentic audience deepens the value of the work students engage in because it communicates that others care about and are invested in their efforts. Although it's a staple element of PBL, I want to expand on it here because it enhances every area of learning.

An authentic audience brings relevancy and meaning to the work students are doing. Let's unpack what this could look like in our classrooms and schools.

Maker Education Sharings

When my students learned that they were going to be sharing about their maker projects from a cardboard box challenge inspired by Caine's Arcade and made on our class YouTube channel, they were ecstatic! Learners had the autonomy to create one of the following, each of which encompassed learning standards:

* A commercial that persuaded others to want to buy their cardboard arcade-style game
* A newscast that informed individuals about what the invention could do and how they came up with their idea
* A skit that served to entertain while incorporating information pertaining to their cardboard arcade creation

Knowing that their YouTube videos could be shared on our class website and social media, thereby increasing who was viewing their work, learners' drive and creativity skyrocketed! The awareness that they'd have an authentic audience compelled them to be intentional about their work and reflective of their product.

In addition to creating and sharing media that depicted what we created during the cardboard box challenge, we took the project to the next level by partnering with Barnes and Noble for their Mini-Maker Faire. Learners and their families arrived one Saturday morning in November to dedicate four hours of time to sharing, demonstrating, and participating with those in attendance as they showcased their cardboard arcade-game-style creations.

Capable at Any Age

Younger learners may require more support initially, but that doesn't have to limit their options for sharing their work with an authentic audience. Lindsey Danhoff, a K–3 teacher, spoke to this with Vickie Davis, teacher, IT Director, and host of *The Cool Cat Teacher* podcast. Danhoff explained that when working with kinder-garten and first-grade students, it is important to list a few sample ideas for sharing knowledge and then let students come up with other choices. Her students, for example, understood that they could make a video, Google slides, a Wixie (a digital page that can create a digital book), a model out of clay, or even a book or a poster.[2] By exposing learners to a variety of options, they develop intrinsic motivation as they tailor their presentation to their personal interests.

Authentic Audience within PBL

I also watched the intrinsic motivation develop firsthand within my oldest son, Julian. During his sixth-grade year, his class was empowered through PBL. Like many other locations in America, our mall has declined as businesses have closed. Considering that we have several empty store locations, Julian's teachers told them that their help was needed to revitalize our mall. They wanted to hear what busi-nesses kids thought would be successful. Within this project, learners had to research stores and activities that would attract customers, and apply mathematics by studying demographic data to learn if the business would fit in the empty store space, and how much it would cost to bring in a store or franchise. Julian's team selected Sky Zone Trampoline Park, as our area could benefit from more children-centered activities. They reasoned that individuals currently have to drive close to one-and-a-half hours to enjoy similar activities, and the business would be successful in our area.

Following their research and learning, the students launched a project expo. Learners from each team even wore shirts featuring logos and had hands-on or food-related experiences based on their business proposal for what should fill the empty store locations in order for community stakeholders to gain a better knowledge of what their business had to offer. For example, Julian's team had the Sky Zone logo printed on shirts and had a basketball and hoop to demonstrate a sample of one activity Sky Zone offers. Another team who was seeking to bring a Mexican chain to our mall served chips and salsa to those who visited their booth. These simple yet creative touches fostered an authentic feel as students pitched their ideas along with supportive research depicting why the businesses would thrive and benefit our community.

The stakeholders who attended included local business owners, bankers, politicians, and other professionals, in addition to parents. Individuals moved around the expo to hear each team's pitch and then completed a rubric for feedback. I recall Julian being so invested and convinced that Sky Zone would be added to our mall, and he was incredibly motivated by this to master learning to make his project pitch successful. An expo is such a great way to connect with community stakeholders.

Top **10** Reasons for Students to Blog

Blogging...

5 Gives students a voice

6 Teaches digital citizenship

4 Showcases student accomplishments

HooRay!

7 Gives students a global and authentic audience

3 Improves writing and digital literacy

My Blog

8 Creates a digital portfolio

2 Establishes a home-school connection

9 Is cross-curricular

MATH
SOCIAL STUDIES
SCIENCE
LANGUAGE ARTS
PHYS ED
DRAMA
MUSIC
VISUAL ARTS

1 Promotes collaboration

10 Develops critical thinking skills

@sylviaduckworth

Blogging to an Authentic Audience

Classroom and student blogs are another way to empower learners to share their experiences with an authentic audience. In addition to the reasons Sylvia Duckworth shares in her Top Ten Reasons for Students to Blog sketchnote, blogging provides a powerful way for learners to reflect on or summarize their learning.

We can support our learners as bloggers in the following ways:

* Share examples of what it could look like.
* Teach about online safety and digital citizenship (best taught in any situation where technology is leveraged).

* Start with simple, low-risk prompts, such as inviting learners to introduce themselves and share about an activity they enjoy.
* Allow time to explore functions in the blog (if accessible in the platform), such as colors, fonts, and themes. This promotes learners to begin identifying who they are and how they want to represent themselves.
* Explore ways to provide effective feedback that is well received. This includes identifying how we can find the strengths within each post, and ask "I wonder" statements.
* Connect with three or four other classes who blog to broaden the audience reach. Doing so provides the opportunity for diversity of ideas and thoughts, but learners still start to get to know one another and gain comfort sharing.
* Invite families to read and comment on blogs. (Tip: Include resources for parents on how to comment appropriately to encourage learners, as this is an opportunity for students to develop their voice and grow as a risk-taker.)
* Avoid connecting a grade to blog posts to encourage learners as creative thinkers and to test their own thoughts on topics of their choice.

Considering that centers provide learners with autonomy in the classroom, one suggestion is to create a blogging station where students blog about their project and then a second station where they comment on their peers' blogs. Provide time for learners to respond to comments at the conclusion, fostering deep reflection and communication. Not only do learners gain practice at reading and writing, but they will also receive authentic feedback. Depending on your structure, there may be opportunities for several classrooms to engage in this process. Blogging and providing feedback are both great activities for learners to engage in when other classwork is complete.

Also, if you have parent volunteers, they can engage as active participants by reading student blogs and leaving comments. An authentic audience through blogging makes learning relevant, which increases intrinsic motivation. Similar options for sharing digitally include posting online learning portfolios and curating student work on a class website. There's not one "right" way to begin; just find an option that works for you and your students, and start sharing!

Empower Learners to Lead Exploration Camps

Student-led sessions, similar to Edcamps for adults, bring authenticity to new heights. They can be incorporated in any content to enhance learning; our teaching team first attempted student-led learning sessions following the completion of our passion projects. We launched "exploration camps," which were all about empowering learners to explore topics that piqued their interests. Students were thrilled to have the opportunity to not only share their learning and passions with their peers, but also to learn from one another. Whereas Edcamps encourage all attendees to participate and provide input, our exploration camps combined a mini-presentation of the project followed by questions and a discussion that involved the voices of all attendees.

The idea spawned upon recognizing that students were curious about the learning and work that their peers were engaged in. Seizing the opportunity to catapult authenticity through exploration camps encouraged all learners to take pride in creating a mini-presentation to engage their peers. Exploration camps are ideal when interwoven within maker education, passion projects, project-based learning, or any scenario where learners can leverage their ability to share learning that is specific to the work they've done. As with infusing all of the components discussed in Part III, I think that, as innovators ourselves, we should always be looking for ways to work sharing opportunities, such as exploration camps, into what we're doing.

Below, I've broken down the steps to setting up an exploration camp. As always, I encourage you to retool and innovate how this looks for your classroom. The goal should be creating dynamic experiences tailored to the unique needs of your learners.

Launching Exploration Camps

1. Tell students that everyone will have the opportunity to demonstrate their learning through exploration camps. Explain that exploration camps involve students sharing what they've learned via a presentation and question-and-answer time with a small group of their peers.

2. Cocreate the expectations and format with students. It will look different at various grade levels and settings. With my students, I emphasize that how they want their presentations to look is completely up to them. They can use PowerPoint, Google Slides, or even create digital media using video or apps to communicate their learning to engage and teach their peers. It's beneficial for learners to understand the expectations regarding showing respect and empathy toward the presenter. This is also a good opportunity to talk with students about embracing a growth mindset throughout the process. Keeping these sessions informal. Maintaining a focus on sharing and discussion as a form of teaching fosters greater risk-taking than the pressure that can accompany formal presentations.

3. Ensure that only a few individuals present at a time and limit the number of attendees who can sign up for a specific

session to ensure all sessions have attendees. When we engage in exploration camps, I carefully select which three students present at the same time as I typically have some idea of where learners will go based on their interests. It's important to ensure that every learner has the opportunity to explore what they're most interested in while also making sure that no session is left empty.

4. Prepare learners to ask quality questions and explain that everyone can participate in the group discussion to deepen learning. It does not have to be the sole responsibility of the presenter to answer every single question; create the opportunity for all members to share their learning and understanding on the topic if applicable.

5. Follow up with a reflection strategy so that learners can process all that they learned from the presentation and discussion.

6. As a next step, connect with another class in your school or virtually with learners from another state or country. Doing so empowers learners as global collaborators. It's exciting for kids to share and learn from peers their age beyond those they're connected with on a regular basis.

When students have the opportunity to choose their learning based on their interests and passions, they take ownership of their education. And when they feel supported through the classroom culture and structures to share what they've learned, they practice essential leaderships skills.

Remaining Open-Minded to Possibilities

If you do a quick search online, you'll find many child entrepreneurs who have successfully created their own businesses. You can also find countless examples of children and teens who are making a tangible and positive difference in their communities around the world. With that in mind, we should never underestimate what our students are capable of. And that means that even when we hear an outlandish idea, we need to keep an open mind.

When you read child entrepreneur success stories, it's often the parents who have helped them to navigate the waters of how to make their vision become a reality. Max Ash is one such child. He had a unique idea to combine his passion for basketball and hot chocolate by creating The Mug With a Hoop™. Ash's invention allows kids to enjoy their tasty drink while having fun shooting marshmallows into the hoop that is attached to the rim of the mug. Ash's mom, Jennifer, explains that Ash, who has dyslexia, is an incredibly creative thinker. "Traditional definitions of success often leave kids like Max behind because they think and learn differently," she says.

Let's unpack that statement for a moment. How do we traditionally define success? Often it's through grades based on homework completion, classroom assignments, and assessments. The truth is, numbers can never truly speak to the capabilities of our learners. If a student receives low grades due to handing in assignments late, and those numbers get averaged into the overall assessment grade, how accurately does that reflect the child's understanding of the subject matter? The answer is that it doesn't, which leaves me wondering whether that age-old practice is a proficient way to summarize what a student understands or has mastered. Some schools have gone grade-less and have moved to observation, feedback, iteration, and student self-evaluation as a means to better gauge the growth of students. The bottom line is that in creating a culture of innovation, we need to have conversations around these topics as traditional definitions of success may actually be hindering growth in learners.

Let's return to Ash's story. His mother explains, "What this experience has taught us is that even if he's not at the top of the echelon when it comes to good grades and strong SAT scores, we don't need to be worried about his career path. So long as he embraces his own creative instincts, people will not only pay him for his art but also for his ideas." Ash's invention has been quite a success and sells at Amazon, Nordstrom, Uncommon Goods, and other retailers. He's making his mark as a child entrepreneur and continues to make progress with the support of his family, outside of school.[3] Ash is fortunate to have his family help him with this endeavor. Every child deserves ample opportunities to explore their interests, as one can never predict what ideas lie within. As educators, carving out time for learners to hone in on their passions is just the tipping point to supporting them in their journey. Just imagine the possibilities if we unleashed the inner creative ideas and talents of the children we work with!

L.E.A.P. Onward

There is no map or pacing guide that dictates the way to empower learning or create authentic experience. We must be the innovators of education for our students and provide them opportunities for exploration. A couple ways to do that include bringing together the components of maker education, passion-infused learning, and project-based learning and empowering students to share their work with larger audiences. These authentic experiences bring value to the work learners have engaged in and allow students to demonstrate and expand on what they have accomplished, created, or discovered. It is through these kinds of authentic and personalized learning experiences that we can best cultivate the skills our students need for success.

L.E.A.P. Tips and Takeaways

* Following learning that infuses elements of maker education, passion-based learning, or project-based learning, carve out time for students to lead exploration camps.
* Leverage your connections in the community and on social media to help connect with an authentic audience to share out to and support students by helping them learn to make these connections.
* Demonstrate unwavering support for every learner. Deep within is potential waiting to be unleashed.

L.E.A.P. beyond Your Boundaries

Share your reflections, questions, and ideas using #LEAPeffect.

1. Why is it important to empower learners as leaders?
2. How could you integrate the concept of exploration camps in your classroom or school?
3. Which organization or business in your community could enhance an area of your curriculum to bring relevance to learning and serve as a community partner?

Chapter 13
Honor Your Impact

If you truly pour your heart into what you
believe in, even if it makes you vulnerable,
amazing things can and will happen.

—Emma Watson

The hit movie *The Greatest Showman* is packed with emotionally charged songs full of passion and inspiration. One song, "This is Me," sung by Keala Settle, has become incredibly popular. A YouTube video of the live behind-the-scenes recording of this anthem reveals the immense synergy felt amongst individuals who collaborated to bring this musical masterpiece to life. In an interview with director Michael Gracey and Settle, they share that the recording captured the very first time Settle sang, "This is Me," as no one had heard her sing it before that moment. To this day it fascinates me to learn from the interview that Settle didn't even want to come out from behind the music stand to sing in front of others. Having watched the movie and listened to the soundtrack numerous times, I initially struggled to look at Settle through a different lens. How could someone who possesses extraordinary talent and appears so confident feel uncomfortable and even scared to step out in front of others in the studio to shine?

I encourage you to take a moment and watch the video to gain the full context:

Keala Settle singing
This is Me for the first time

Gracey recalls encouraging her that day by saying, "Just step out because this is your moment, you have to step out into the ring metaphorically because that's what you're doing and you've got to stand in front of everyone and just belt it out." In response, Settle explains, "And I didn't want to. In fact, I stood behind the music stand until the day of that presentation. There was a moment in the song that I actually was so scared that I had to grab onto Hugh's (Hugh Jackman) hand so that I had somebody to hold on to. Then, we got to the end of the number, and all I remember is a deafening, deafening applause."

Have you ever felt so scared or nervous to step out of your zone of comfort or embrace vulnerability? Fearing failure, ridicule, or perhaps the uneasiness of change?

I'm certain we've all felt this way at one time or another in life. Change is hard, but with change, we can make what may seem impossible, possible. Fear inhibits creativity, thus affecting how well we can spark a culture of innovation in our schools. If you recall from Part I, a luminous culture is what promotes us to develop as risk-takers and unleash creativity through divergent thinking. A luminous culture encourages people to shine in the face of fear.

In watching the recording of Settle, what stood out most to me is how she starts off behind the stand, visibly timid. The more Settle progresses through the lyrics, she gradually begins to take one step forward at a time. Settle steps out just as she courageously sings with deep, raw emotion that she's marching on to the beat she drums.

Journeying through this book, my hope is that you'll feel more equipped to take the L.E.A.P. Dare to march on to your own beat as it contributes to the melody of the shared vision of your school or district. We've explored the importance of fostering a luminous culture and ways to do so, strategies and tips to best empower learning, and ways in which we can infuse authenticity through meaningful learning experiences. I challenge each of us to step out, and move forward, to ensure we nurture the growth of ourselves and others. Stepping forward demonstrates that we honor our inner potential and recognize the impact we can make individually *and* collectively on education. Stepping forward also encourages those with whom we're connected to join the movement. Have the courage to embrace your strengths and talents along with the impact that comes as a result. I don't know of any scenario in which one individual drove a movement alone. Those who have cultivated change had someone who either inspired and encouraged them or had others who joined in their mission due to feeling moved by their drive and cause. One such

Dare to march on to your own beat as it contributes to the melody of the shared vision of your school or district.

world changer leading the charge for education in her own way is Malala Yousafzai.

In 2008, the Taliban infiltrated Swat Valley, Pakistan, exerting rigid rules, along with unmerciful consequences, turning civilian lives upside down. Demonstrating their power and reigning with terror, the Taliban attacked education in Swat Valley, with an emphasis on female education. Throughout their attack, almost 184 schools were bombed, with approximately 120 of them schools for girls.[1]

Despite the undeniable risk, Malala courageously spoke out, advocating for all girls to receive an education. Malala is a prime example of someone who could have very easily backed into comfort by accepting life as determined by the Taliban. She shares, "I loved school. But everything changed when the Taliban took control of our town in Swat Valley. The extremists banned many things—like owning a television and playing music—and enforced harsh punishments for those who defied their orders. And they said girls could no longer go to school. In January 2008, when I was just eleven years old, I said goodbye to my classmates, not knowing when—if ever—I would see them again."

I can't even comprehend the fear that Malala and her peers must have experienced. Despite the threats, Malala continued to step forward to honor her impact. Malala boldly spoke publicly declaring her right, along with the right of all girls, to receive an education. Speaking out was bold and courageous.

Unfortunately, this act made Malala a target. Malala recalls, "In October 2012, on my way home from school, a masked gunman boarded my school bus and asked, 'Who is Malala?' He shot me on the left side of my head." It's a miracle that Malala survived this brutal attack. Again, it would be so easy for Malala to retreat to remain safe. How many of us would continue forward?

But Malala is incredibly resilient. She states, "It was then I knew I had a choice: I could live a quiet life, or I could make the most of this new life I had been given. I determined to continue my fight until every girl could go to school." Malala, from the time she was born, always had her father as an ally and inspiration. She even went on to establish the Malala Fund, to support females to achieve their dreams, and was the recipient of the Nobel Peace Prize in December 2014.[2]

Having the courage to step out, embrace your talents, and remain true to your beliefs could have immense impact beyond the walls of your own classroom, potentially positively affecting hundreds or thousands more students.

Returning to Settle, an example of the power of one person making a move occurs in that recording room. She is surrounded by backup vocalists and musicians playing various instruments. While all musicians are engaged and contributing to the makeup of this song, they gain compelling momentum as Settle gathers inner strength. When she steps into her power, passion erupts for everyone in the room. I've watched the recording 100 times, easily, because the dynamics that ensue fascinate me! In the moment when Settle embraces her fear and turns it into courage, others in the studio tear up, smile in awe, energetically dance to the beat, and belt out the lyrics with rich, deep emotion as they get caught up in the experience right along with her. And, as I listen, I am drawn into the contagious brilliance of their moment.

Ultimately, this is my vision for our schools. I desire us to honor our impact by stepping out and being vulnerable to take responsible risks. Let's get crazily jazzed up about what we're doing, and embrace taking the L.E.A.P. little by little. In doing so, we create the potential of a ripple effect that inspires others to L.E.A.P. too, creating irresistible synergy, just as Settle did. Summarizing the recorded experience, Gracey states that it's "a moment that will stay with him the rest of his life." Honor your impact and all you have to offer. Collaboratively

Honor your impact and all you have to offer. Collaboratively create moments that will stay with you, your colleagues, and most importantly your students for the rest of their lives.

create moments that will stay with you, your colleagues, and most importantly your students for the rest of their lives. Settle exudes inspiration and passion as she sings. In turn, all others followed her lead. When people feel energy of this magnitude flowing from a leader, they will often follow by modeling it.[3]

Courage is the resistance to fear, mastery of fear, *not* absence of fear.

—Mark Twain

We've all experienced a time when we've held back in some capacity from doing what we desire as a result of fear, doubt, or perhaps nervousness, as discussed in Part I. Deep within, we *all* have courage, and we choose daily to evoke it or allow it to remain dormant inside us. Tapping into our own strengths serves as the foundation for honoring our impact and stepping out to influence others. Many schools utilize StrengthsFinder 2.0 to better identify the depth

We all have courage, and we choose daily to evoke it or allow it to remain dormant inside us.

of strengths pertaining to individuals and what they naturally do best. This resource provides feedback on our influence, ability to connect through relationships, and how we think about and analyze information and situations.

A sample of just some of the many strengths that we may readily recognize in ourselves or our colleagues may include the following:

* Connecting with learners through relationships
* Questioning techniques
* Engagement strategies
* Ways we empower students
* Integrating technology in meaningful ways
* Planning and organization leading to implementation

We need to intentionally seek opportunities to build up one another and give energy. As Kara Knollmeyer, educational leader and author of *Unleash Talent*, writes, "The truth is, our words, talents, and our time have the power to change another person's life for the better."

If you're seeking commitment to a vision that is crafted and supported by all voices, inspire those you're connected with through influence and by inspiring them to unleash their strengths by adding value to them.

Let's dive into the story of Settle's debut to further explore through a different lens. Some individuals may express that they perceived the scenario differently. While the musicians certainly gained momentum and expressed deeper emotion throughout their performance as a result of Settle stepping out, many acknowledge that the more passionate the musicians became, Settle was provoked to dig even deeper for courage as a product of their support and inspiration in return. Settle brought her stardom because she was pushed by others who recognized her talent. It's very possible that Settle may not have stepped out without encouragement from others.

Likewise, we have talent that exists within the four walls of many classrooms where it's comfortable. Not only should we be stepping out but uplifting others and encouraging them to step out as well. Synergy energizes us to continue onward.

Just as observed in the recording of Settle, one person doesn't typically create a musical masterpiece independently. Every vocalist, instrumentalist, composer, and studio creative who offers collective ideas and contributions brings compelling vibrancy that uplifts through music. There is something compelling about music that creates a wave of emotion and inspiration. How can we replicate that feeling in our schools by doing the right work with kids?

Remember what's most important isn't how far we're stepping outside our comfort zone, but that we're continually taking steps to grow beyond our boundaries. Every one of us can encompass the qualities of a leader to spark the movement. Leadership is influence, and we cultivate this by sharing our why, inspiring others to take action, and asking individuals to help us by contributing their strengths.

Take time to reflect on the following:

* How can you harness your strengths and unleash talent to create your desired impact?
* What additional learning do you require to help you reach your goal?
* What obstacles exist that you need support overcoming and how can you "innovate in the box" given the constraints?
* How can you inspire others to take action?
* What are your areas of growth, and how can you add value to those you work alongside and leverage their strengths?
* Who do you consider members of your tribe? Who pushes and inspires your thinking?

These questions can also be used with students and modified depending on their age. We want our kids to grow up knowing that they, too, can have influence leading to impact—rather than thinking that their role is to be passive learners who accept that school is something done to them. This can be game-changing for both kids and adults. Let's explore these questions more deeply.

Desired Impact

Knowing your desired impact serves as a guide to help navigate your journey. It's critical that we return to our why before taking the L.E.A.P. and retool along the way when something doesn't go as planned. We can have a desired impact through a shared vision and even for day-to-day learning. As education continues to evolve, your desired impact will understandably shift. There are also serendipitous moments that result unexpectedly as a result of our efforts to reach our desired impact.

An example of this is when Rachel Lamb, Steven Thomas, and I had the desired impact of developing global communicators and empowered learning for students through the virtual connection of our New York and New Mexico classes as discussed in Chapter 5. Our intended outcome was for learners to use Design Thinking to create a prototype that replicated the purpose of the contraption that allowed the Mars Rover to land safely on Mars. Learners in our classes replicated this scenario through an egg-drop challenge.

For me, the serendipitous moment occurred following our initial meeting. Born was an inquiry-based learning opportunity that infused the interests of students on the topic of outer space. It all stemmed from learning tidbits about the Mars Rover through our virtual project launch. Rather than sticking solely to our plan, we went off route and developed modified passion projects that sprouted from curiosity about space! Learners created their own map and took a deeper dive into their learning than if I'd solely stuck to my original plan. We still collaborated in the STEAM challenge through Design Thinking, but also carved out time for students to take their learning in a direction of their own choice. You can do this by utilizing chunks of time in a day, or dedicating time once per week, and embedding learning standards to ensure it's doable. What I learned was to seize opportunities that arise, leading to a greater impact on learning.

Harness Your Strengths, Unleash Talent

Each of us is unique. I know where my strengths and areas of talents lie, just as much as I recognize the areas in which I require growth. If our schools become fixated on programs and mandates, we lose the personal touches that individuals bring to the table. Seek to embrace the strengths and talents of those you work alongside, then add value by building upon them. One person may see the big picture but struggle to bring together the nuts and bolts to articulate it. Diverse teams have the potential to catapult us forward. Tap into strengths by providing time for individuals to consider the vision and how they can infuse their talent to bring insurmountable opportunities to the school and learners.

Embrace Learning

With your goal in mind, what learning do you require? If we can identify the area in which we need growth to spark the impact we desire, our journey becomes more intentional. Creating the conditions that foster a culture of learning, where educators engage in and share learning together, propels us forward and leads to improved opportunities for our kids. Tara Martin, administrator, and author of *Be R.E.A.L.* shares a thought-provoking quote in her blog from the book

Show Your Work by Austin Kleon: "The world is changing at such a rapid rate that it's turning us all into amateurs. Even for professionals, the best way to flourish is to retain an amateur's spirit and embrace uncertainty and the unknown."[4] Take a moment to think about that. When interviewing me for a new role, the committee asked what expertise I could bring to their school. After sharing my strengths and talents, I proceeded to share that I hope to have the opportunity to work alongside individuals who push and challenge my thinking because I'm well aware that in any role in education, we must seek continuous learning, leading to growth, as change is a constant.

Obstacles Create Conditions for Innovation

While there may be obstacles that we can overcome, often constraints exist that we cannot change. How often have you heard educators say, "If we had a bigger budget," or "If state testing was eliminated," and "If more time existed." Perhaps you've said this yourself; I know I have. The reality is that we can wish all we want and even participate as advocates for kids to create change in these areas. However, in the meantime, it's crucial that we don't sit back and simply wish, but look for opportunities to move forward. We can create a culture of innovation by embedding the components of Parts II and III within any area of learning. Embedding learning standards and desired success skills provide the end goal. How we get there is up to us, and we can innovate learning using Design Thinking to create top-notch learning experiences for kids. Trust that you and your team, in addition to those within your professional learning network, can and will successfully innovate inside the box as strengths and talents are leveraged.

What Hinders People from Honoring Their Impact	Ways to Honor Your Impact
Fear of what others may think about their ideas (concerned about ridicule or isolation)	• Trust that your ideas may lead to something incredible. • Share your thoughts with trusted individuals and engage in learning to strengthen your idea. • Intentionally go out of your way to add value to colleagues to increase their confidence.
Lack of support	• Within your own school or district, share your ideas with trusted colleagues who are likely to be a support system. • Find your tribe on social media and team with educators from around the world.
Stuck in old paradigms, i.e., not enough time, money, etc.	• Challenge yourself to rethink your structures to utilize time and money more efficiently, and that will have a direct impact on student growth. • Rethink your structure for more integration focusing on skills-based instruction. • Pool your resources with colleagues, i.e., complete supply orders collaboratively with teammates in order to share.

Feeling safe in their comfort zone	• Set a goal to attempt a L.E.A.P. tip that will push you outside of your comfort zone. • Connect with a trusted colleague or someone in your professional learning network to work toward a common L.E.A.P. tip.

Adding Value and Leveraging Strengths

To foster a culture where each individual is encouraged to honor their impact, add value by intentionally commenting on the strengths of those you work alongside. Take time to recognize their efforts. Feeling celebrated or even simply acknowledged encourages us to continue pursuing growth. Likewise, when we demonstrate vulnerability and seek help from colleagues, we gain their unique perspective and craft deeper learning experiences for students, as opposed to when we simply offer up our own help. Igniting a culture of innovation requires us to not simply take the L.E.A.P. ourselves but to embrace vulnerability by seeking a boost from others as they can springboard us forward—while also serving as a support system for others as well.

Find Your Tribe, Connect on Social Media

Most educators are eager to help others to be successful. Finding your tribe locally and on social media can be transformational. When I first joined Twitter, I was completely unaware of how many phenomenal educators would be eager to connect and link arms to collectively move forward for the sake of our youth. Many people begin through simple interactions such as reading and commenting or retweeting blog posts that inspire or challenge their thinking. Additionally, there are Twitter chats accessible for every educator. Identify your area of passion or growth and find a chat to join. Facebook and Instagram also have spaces to connect and grow alongside others. Connecting through social media has the potential to propel your growth as you share ideas, resources, and network with others.

L.E.A.P. Onward

Honoring your impact, as Keala Settle did when she stepped out to sing "This is Me," empowers us to embrace our strengths and what we have to offer to those we serve. It's okay to demonstrate vulnerability by seeking help and connecting with others to propel your growth.

Imagine how education would shift and, more importantly, the impact it would have on students if every educator was actively seeking to harness a talent as opposed to just doing their job. At the very least, we should be the ones who lift up and support the talent of those who are inspiring others with talents—just as the many backup musicians, actors, and producers did to push Settle further. Celebrate your steps toward growth and those you are connected with as well. Each of us has something remarkable to contribute; how influential will your impact be?

L.E.A.P. Tips and Takeaways

* You are a difference maker; unleash and leverage your strengths and talents to step out.
* Embrace your role as a continuous learner, promoting your growth.

* Add value by recognizing the strengths and talents of others and identifying ways they can be leveraged to accelerate the shared vision.
* Connect with educators on social media, engage in chats, and make authentic connections to continue growing yourself.

L.E.A.P. beyond Your Boundaries

Share your reflections, questions, and ideas using #LEAPeffect.

1. How will you encourage an open culture where individuals honor their impact and strengths/talents are leveraged?
2. What opportunities could be provided to encourage the continued improvement of current strengths and talents while nurturing learning in our areas of growth?

Chapter 14

Initiate the L.E.A.P.

Here's to the crazy ones. The misfits. The rebels. The troublemakers. The round pegs in the square holes. The ones who see things differently. They're not fond of rules. And they have no respect for the status quo. You can quote them, disagree with them, glorify or vilify them. About the only thing you can't do is ignore them. Because they change things. They push the human race forward. And while some may see them as the crazy ones, we see genius. Because the people who are crazy enough to think they can change the world, are the ones who do.

—Rob Siltanen

The creative folks at Pixar eat, sleep, and breathe storytelling. It is the lifestyle they live as they diligently craft films that capture our hearts and stir our emotions. All of their movies, crafted with complex technology and planning, begin with an idea that is brainstormed and built on by this dedicated team.

After watching "Pixar in a Box," tutorials created by Pixar in collaboration with Khan Academy that depicts the storytelling process, I couldn't help but make connections between cultivating innovation in our schools and Pixar's filmmaking process. Clearly, there are distinct differences, but like the stories Pixar tells, innovation within our schools—particularly when innovating what we're currently doing or crafting something entirely new in connection with the needs and interests of our learners—begins with an idea.

Innovation Thrives with Many Voices

At Pixar, ideas take shape as stories. Then the director, writers, and artists collaboratively figure out what happens in each story through the creation of simple drawings. During the film-creation process, production designers create the world and characters while storyboards go to editorial, where everything including music, dialogue, and sound effects get strung together and timed out. Animators then use computer programing to move the characters in a digital world, and technical artists problem-solve how to create the movie within computers using science, mathematics, and coding. Each file requires a myriad of roles and expertise. Similarly, to bring ideas for innovation and empowering experiences to life in our schools, it's critical to employ an array of voices and talents. We can leverage the diverse expertise and passions of community stakeholders, colleagues, students, and our professional learning networks.[1]

We Must Take Action

Ideas carry the potential for limitless possibilities in creating purposeful learning experiences that ignite a culture of innovation. But ideas alone don't lead to immediate change. Questions may arise and lead to hesitancy. Resistance may surface in response to ideas and the possibilities that accompany them. Change can evoke fear and cause people to want to revert back to familiarity. But opposition is not a reason to stop pursuing innovative, engaging, and empowered learning for our students. Just as we want our students to demonstrate a growth mindset, we, too, must maintain a steadfast commitment to cultivating authentic relationships and engaging in intentional collaboration in order to make our vision a reality.

When fostering a culture of innovation, there will be moments when shifts feel sticky. Truth be told, on occasion, our efforts will result in what feels like a failure; but remember, we cannot and will not wave our white flag and surrender to the status quo. We must choose to see failure as an opportunity to dig deep inside, learn from the experiences, and muster our tenacity to retool and sharpen our efforts.

If you look around, particularly on social media, you may feel frustrated and be tempted to believe that some educators are flawlessly successful in their quest to transform their learning culture. Remember that beneath every success exists bumps and bruises from the tumultuous journey. Adam Grant, author of *Originals*, shares on the topic of successful risk-taking individuals: "They feel the same fear, the same self-doubt, as the rest of us. What sets them apart is that they take action anyway. They know in their hearts that failing would yield less regard than failing to try."[2] Collectively, we can overcome the doubts, fears, and resistance as we build trust with each step we take toward better education for our students. Together, we must take action.

Exhibit Tenacity

Throughout the various stages of film production at Pixar, the scenes they create are updated or retooled repeatedly. Considering that Pixar continually refines their work throughout the entire operation, and a single frame can take twenty-four hours or more to create (depending on the stumbling blocks they encounter), it's clear that a growth mindset is required to persevere through the unpredictable process. It's probable that some mistakes may even lead to innovative new ideas. But just imagine the celebration that occurs when the final masterpiece is released! It's vital—no matter what obstacles we have to go under, over, or through—that we proceed even as we reflect and revise along the way.

I watch my own children as they strive to create, solve, or accomplish a task just as they envision on the first try; but that's rarely how things go. Often, they'll express frustration and even want to quit. That's when my husband, Michael, and I step in and encourage them to remember that nothing great ever comes without effort. If it's easy, it isn't memorable or seems to lack value. So when students complete an assignment, receive a grade, and then move on to the next task without much effort, it's not surprising that they don't remember much of what they've learned. By crafting relevant and meaningful learning through various avenues discussed within this book, we can provide learners with the opportunities to develop future success skills—including reflection and revision—that are essential to cultivating the idea that learning is intricate and ceaseless.

Within our work in education, the filmmaking process at Pixar, and in countless business situations, "one and done" doesn't exist. Well, not if we're truly invested in the process of creating a sustainable work of art through the inspiration of our vision. Taking the L.E.A.P. to ignite a culture of innovation requires us, along with our learners, to embrace the concept that learning is a continuous journey.

You're the Author of the Future Chapters within Your Story

We started this book by exploring our own personal narratives. Each of us has a unique story that has contributed to who we are today. But we are the authors, creators, and designers of our future chapters.

Moving forward to initiate the L.E.A.P., what will the future chapters of your story look like?

What ideas are you inspired to bring to life?

If you aren't sure, you can spark ideas by asking, "What if . . . ?" What if questions invoke imagination, and as Pixar storyboard artist Kristen Lester shares, "The best 'what ifs' are questions that feel like a key that unlocks a door."

It's time to unlock the door to a culture of innovation where learners are empowered within a student-centered learning environment and where the 6Cs of reimagining learning thrive, cultivating the essential future success skills.

Asking, "What if . . . " initiates our L.E.A.P.

Take a moment to pause and reflect on your own "what if" questions around igniting a culture of innovation. Write down as many as you can. Then, with a team, share your thoughts. This activity requires us to demonstrate vulnerability as we want to promote others to engage in divergent thinking to unleash ideas that have the potential to propel us forward. It also compels us to listen to others' voices. Remember that innovation thrives with many voices, so devote the time to truly listen to others' ideas, regardless of their position, years of service, or popularity.

Perhaps as you put ideas together, new or improved approaches will sprout. Nurturing our ideas and allowing time for them to germinate ensures that they blossom. As with innovation itself, our ideas will likely grow in various directions, just as a plant grows toward sunlight. As the needs of learners shift, our ideas do as well.

Filled with Promise

We all possess immense inner potential, and we have the choice to leverage it to take the L.E.A.P. and bring the very best learning opportunities to our students.

Likewise, every child comes to us filled with promise and potential. It's our obligation to inspire our learners and serve as guides as they navigate their journeys—not to push them through the system simply to consume content.

Rather than asking kids what they want to *be* when they grow up, let's start asking questions like, "What purpose would you like to serve?" or "What impact would you like to have?" With this approach—and by helping them discover their interests and passions—we can help them find their purpose and tap into the unlimited potential within them. That's how we will effect positive influence on the minds of our learners.

None of us can predict what the children we are entrusted with will become. And there are countless examples of how we need to be cautious not to underestimate the potential of any child or make assumptions about what they'll become in life. Take a look at the Twitter post from Alexandra Penfold, author of six children's books:

Alexandra Penfold @AgentPenfold · 5d
This weekend I sorted through some papers my mom saved from my childhood. The top one is my 4th grade self evaluation. The bottom, my 4th grade state test score. Random House published my 6th book last week. #MoreThanATest

> Writing I love to write and I hope to become an author someday.

4th grade self evaluation vs. state test

WRITING SAMPLE	STUDENT SCORE
Holistic Writing Score (Remedial Standard is 4 of 8) (Writing Goal is 7 of 8)	4
This student is minimally proficient in writing.	

If she believed the state test, Alexandra might never have become an author. Yes, assessment is part of teaching today, but rather than letting the test have the final say, let's recognize it for what it is: a singular measure of our multifaceted, multitalented, and promise-filled students.

Begin Your Quest to L.E.A.P.

I began the quest to take the L.E.A.P. because of some of my own schooling experiences in addition to those of our sons. I'm optimistic that we can collectively create experiences that foster authentic learning opportunities in all schools so that our youth can identify and connect with what matters to them. My hope is that we strive to inspire learners to honor their impact and take action. I'm grateful for educators who spark curiosity and motivation in learners, and we've been fortunate also to experience numerous teachers who have done just that. Together, I believe we can make it more prevalent.

Throughout this book, I've shared the importance of starting small and then layering on new strategies, protocols, or components described throughout each chapter. Education is an ongoing work of progress; we will never be "finished" with innovation. That means there's no pressure to incorporate everything immediately. Change is gradual and can be messy, and that's okay! When we each take on the role of innovator, we can craft learning that is authentic, engaging, and empowering to our students.

You may wonder, *What now*? To reach your full potential through taking the L.E.A.P., start by reflecting on where you are currently. That's your starting point. Then identify your desired impact. Let the acronym L.E.A.P. guide you as you lay the groundwork that will help you successfully launch your efforts.

You picked up this book because of your desire to be an agent of change. You know education can be better for your students. *Now* is the time to create improved opportunities and experiences, and the sky's the limit!

Ready? L.E.A.P.!

"It's impossible," said pride.

"It's risky," said experience.

"It's pointless," said reason.

"Give it a try," whispered the heart.

—Unknown

With Deep Appreciation and Gratitude

When I step back and reflect on the process of writing this book and all the moments that led up to it, I picture the many individuals who have influenced my journey. There are those who shared insights, others who coached or inspired me, and numerous individuals who have encouraged and supported me along the way. I am eternally grateful for each of you.

To my husband, Michael, you have played a pivotal role in my life in more ways than I can count. We met at the State University of Cortland, and it was your enthusiasm and vision for education that contributed to the spark that started me down this very path. Throughout the years, you have challenged my thinking and continue to serve as a thought partner. We are an excellent example of how iron sharpens iron. I am overcome with gratitude that you supported me throughout the writing process, even when your schedule was overflowing with your own obligations. I admire your strength, intelligence, and the way you make me smile. Most of all, I have a deep appreciation for your dedication to our family and the love you demonstrate daily. Your school community is fortunate to have you serving them because I see how immensely you care about the success of not only the learners, but also the teachers you work alongside and their well-being. Seeing your passion shine through inspires me to continue striving to put forth my best.

To my parents, I admire you for your ongoing encouragement, celebration, and support. Each of you has contributed to my growth throughout the years in various ways, influencing who I am today. Mom, you have instilled Sisu in me, passed down by my grandmother, Mary. Sisu is a Finnish concept defined by SisuLab as "extraordinary determination, courage, and resoluteness in the face of extreme adversity. An action mindset which enables individuals to reach beyond their present limitations, take action against all the odds, and transform barriers into frontiers."[1] From the time I was young, you've encouraged my independence and been a constant in my life. I'm grateful for how you listen and intentionally use reflective questioning to guide me to my own decisions. You live your life giving more to others than you seek in return. Your generosity is recognized, and I admire how you walk through life. Thank you for being a positive force in my life and your grandsons' lives.

I have had the honor to work alongside and collaborate with numerous inspirational educators. Karen Bracey, we only worked together for a short time, but your impact was enormous. We connected over our passion for "shaking up the way it's always been done," and you demonstrated how to lead with grace and influence. You encouraged me to "dream big" and "shoot for the stars" with all that I do. Your contagious energy remains with me today, and I hope you're living up your retirement years. To my teammates, Stephanie Andrus, Jamie Dauphinet, and Jessica Shutter, not only have you strengthened my craft, but many lessons shared in this book are a product of our discovery and reflection. We each have varying strengths, and I appreciate how we've complemented one another and always maintained focus on the learners. Our collaboration has always yielded high impact as well as good times filled with immense laughter. I am honored to have worked alongside such phenomenal educators and to be able to genuinely call you my friends. I want to acknowledge all other educators who I have collaborated and worked with for teaching me invaluable lessons that I continue to apply to all areas of life. Alongside you, I have learned the importance of adding value to others, celebrating accomplishments, and removing obstacles to encourage growth in others.

Thank you to every single educator who influenced me as I grew into adulthood, particularly Mrs. Jacqueline Egger, my second-grade teacher. You are someone who made every child feel like somebody. Also, many heartfelt thanks to the professors in the education and psychology departments at The State University of Cortland especially, Timothy Slekar, PhD.

With a warm heart, I extend appreciation for *every single* student I have had the honor to teach and facilitate learning for and alongside. You have all taught me what works best for kids and ways to demonstrate understanding by sharing your ideas. Together, we've created dynamic learning experiences. I appreciate your hugs, smiles, notes, and willingness to open up to me when you needed someone to be there for you. Even after you leave my class, you'll always be considered one of my "kids."

To my dear friend, LaVonna Roth. Our connection formed instantaneously and continues to grow. I have profound gratitude for your mentorship and partnership, and it's a great honor to work alongside you. Your influence is far-reaching, and I continue to learn from your life lessons as you coach me in various ways. Above all, I am blessed with your amazing friendship.

Within my professional learning network, endless encouragement, support, and thought partners exist. I wouldn't miss the opportunity to recognize each of you. I am grateful for my @LeadUpNow tribe and #EdWriteNow families. I admire each of you for your vision for education, support, and willingness to push boundaries. You inspire me to pursue excellence through elevating our field and giving back to the greater good. Heidi Veal and Laura Gilchrist, your partnership with #LeadUpTeach is appreciated, and I thank you both for your inspiration and friendship. Additionally, I want to give a shout-out to all of my friends and family who have offered encouragement along this journey, particularly my dear friend, Beth Gibson, whom I deeply admire, and my sister, Christina Russell, who inspires me to be a difference maker in our world.

A special thanks to the Public Broadcasting Station (PBS) and all PBS Digital Innovators for contributing to my growth. I am honored to be awarded the PBS New York State Digital Innovator Award in addition to the PBS Digital Innovator All-Star Award. However, what I have received regarding professional learning, unmatched experiences, connections, and friendships over the years have been invaluable.

And, to the IMPress and DBC Publishing team—George, Paige, Erin, Dave, and Shelley—thank you from the bottom of my heart for believing in me and helping me to craft this book to share my message. Throughout the entire process, you've served as a support system. You each challenge my thinking, encourage, and inspire me to improve continuously. I am grateful for your communication, vision for education, and creating opportunities for passionate educators to share their voices to inspire others. You are each making a marked impact on education and, in turn, our students.

Notes

Introduction

1. Couros, George. The Innovator's Mindset. San Diego: Dave Burgess Consulting, Inc., 2015, 33.

2. Land, George and Beth Jarman. Breakpoint and Beyond: Mastering the Future Today. New York: HarperBusiness, 1998.

3. Land, George. "The Failure of Success," TedXTucson. February 16, 2011, video, 13:04, youtube.com/watch?v=ZfKMq-rYtnc&feature=youtu.be.

Chapter 1

1. Beck, Julie. "Life's Stories," The Atlantic. August 10, 2015. Accessed September 24, 2018. theatlantic.com/health/archive/2015/08/life-stories-narrative-psychology-redemption-mental-health/400796.

2. "Professional Learning That Shifts Practice," LeadUpTeach, Filmed Feb 23, 2017. YouTube Video, 33:35. youtube.com/watch?v=vdivolJlJmo&t=263s.

3. Martin, Katie. "Teachers Create What They Experience," TEDxElCajonSalon, Filmed May 10, 2016. YouTube video, 8:59. youtube.com/watch?v=rcDpDPwRxvU.

4. King, Hope and Wade King. Wild Card. San Diego: Dave Burgess Consulting, Inc. January 2018.

5. Welcome, Adam and Todd Nesloney, "Kids Deserve It," Episode 69, Filmed April 20, 2017. YouTube video, 19:40. youtube.com/watch?v=rlO7s_Kzcbk.

Chapter 2

1. Sheninger, Eric C. and Thomas C. Murray. Learning Transformed: 8 Keys to Designing Tomorrow's Schools, Today. Virginia: ASCD Publishers, 2017.

2. Sinek, Simon. Start with Why: How Great Leaders Inspire Everyone to Take Action. New York: Penguin Group, 2009, 111.

3. Gray, Alex. "The 10 Skills You Need to Thrive in the Fourth Industrial Revolution," World Economic Forum, January 19, 2016, weforum.org/agenda/2016/01/the-10-skills-you-need-to-thrive-in-the-fourth-industrial-revolution/.

4. Casas, Jimmy. Culturize: Every Student. Every Day. Whatever It Takes. San Diego: Dave Burgess Consulting, Inc., November 2017, 59.

5.   Rose, Todd. The End of Average: How We Succeed in a World That Values Sameness. New York: HarperOne, January 2016.

Chapter 3

1.   Willis, Judy M.D. Research-Based Strategies to Ignite Student Learning, Minnesota: ASCD, 2016, 58.

2.   Branson, Richard. "Why Entrepreneurs Struggle with Formal Education," Virgin. Accessed October 13, 2018. virgin.com/entrepreneur/ richard-branson-why-entrepreneurs-struggle-with-formal-education.

3.   Boaler, Jo. Mathematical Mindsets: Unleashing Students' Potential through Creative Math, Inspiring Messages and Innovative Teaching. San Francisco: Jossey-Bass 2016, 11-13.

4.   "What Is Morning Meeting," Responsive Classroom, 2016. Accessed October 13, 2018. responsiveclassroom.org/what-is-morning-meeting/.

5.   Hill, Bethany. "Let's Take a Walk and Talk About It," December 2017. Accessed October 13, 2018. bethanyshill.com/2017/12/27/ lets-take-a-walk-and-talk-about-it/.

Chapter 4

1.   Couros, George. The Innovator's Mindset. San Diego: Dave Burges Consulting, Inc., October 2015, 2.

2.   Snelling, Jennifer. "The Workforce of the Future," Empowered Learner: A Publication of the International Society for Technology in Education, 11, no.3, January 2018, 21.

3.   Casas, Jimmy. Culturize: Every Student. Every Day. Whatever It Takes. San Diego: Dave Burgess Consulting, Inc., November 22, 2017, 63.

4.   Ross, John A. and Catherine D. Bruce. "Effects of Professional Development on Teacher Efficacy. Results of a Randomized Field Trial," April 2007. legacy. oise.utoronto.ca/research/field-centres/ross/Ross-Bruce%20AERA07.pdf.

5.   Hattie, John. "Hattie Ranking: 252 Influences And Effect Sizes Related To Student Achievement," Visible Learning, December 2017. visible-learning. org/hattie-ranking-influences-effect-sizes-learning-achievement/.

6.   edcamp.org.

Chapter 5

1.   Godin, Seth. Stop Stealing Dreams. What Is School For? sethgodin.typepad. com/files/stop-stealing-dreams-print.pdf, 59.

2. "Girl Launches MIT Admission Letter to Near Space, Video From Space," Filmed February 7th, 2012. Video, YouTube, 8:26. youtube.com/watch?v=hxGF1hmhyJs.

3. Wettrick, Don. "Preparing for a Future that Exists." EdStartup. futurereadyu.com.

4. Martin, Katie. Learner Centered Innovation: Spark Curiosity, Ignite Passion and Unleash Genius. London: Impress, February 6th, 2018, 168.

5. "A Transformational Vision for Education in the US," Education Reimagined, 2015. education-reimagined.org/wp-content/uploads/2015/10/A-Transformational-Vision-for-Education-in-the-US-2015-09.pdf.

6. Richardson, Will. "Curiosity Is the Cat," February 11th, 2017. willrichardson.com/curiosity-is-the-cat/.

Chapter 6

1. "Amelia Earhart Biography," CMG Worldwide. Accessed October 14, 2018. ameliaearhart.com/biography/.

2. "10 Facts About Amelia Earhart," The Children's Museum of Indianapolis, March 23, 2015. childrensmuseum.org/blog/10-facts-about-amelia-earhart.

3. Hurley, Katie. "The Dark Side of Classroom Behavior Management Charts," The Washington Post. September 29, 2016. washingtonpost.com/news/parenting/wp/2016/09/29/the-darkside-of-classroom-behavior-management-charts.

4. Gotbaum, Rachel. "LISTEN: How a 'Drop-out Factory' Turned into Model for Success," The Hechinger Report. October 14, 2017. Accessed October 14, 2018. hechingerreport.org/listen-drop-factory-turned-model-success/.

5. Azzam, Amy M. "Motivated to Learn: A Conversation with Daniel Pink," ACSD, September 2014. Accessed October 13, 2018. ascd.org/publications/educational-leadership/sept14/vol72/num01/Motivated-to-Learn@-A-Conversation-with-Daniel-Pink.aspx.

6. Spencer, John. "Ten Ways to Leverage Student Choice in Your Classroom," August 3, 2016. spencerauthor.com/ten-ways-to-leverage-student-choice-in-your-classroom/.

7. Ferlazzo, Larry. "Response: Student Goal-Setting in the Classroom," Education Week Teacher, January 14, 2017. blogs.edweek.org/teachers/classroom_qa_with_larry_ferlazzo/2017/01/student-goal-setting-in-the-classroom.html.

8. Connell, Genia. "Smart Goal Planner," Scholastic. scholastic.com/content/dam/teachers/blogs/genia-connell/migrated-files/smart_goal_planner.pdf.

Chapter 7

1. Willis, Judy M.D. Research-Based Strategies to Ignite Student Learning, Minnesota: ASCD, 2016, 24.
2. Willis, Judy M.D. Research-Based Strategies to Ignite Student Learning, Minnesota: ASCD, 2016, 24.
3. Winter, Amos and Vijay Govindarajan. "Engineering Reverse Innovations," Harvard Business Review, July-August 2015. hbr.org/2015/07/engineering-reverse-innovations.

Chapter 8

1. Livni, Ephrat. "'Find Your Passion Is Bad Advice,' Say Yale-NUS and Stanford Psychologists," Quartz, June 26, 2018. qz.com/1314088/find-your-passion-is-bad-advice-say-yale-and-stanford-psychologists.
2. Couros, George. "Personalized Learning Vs. Personalization of Learning," The Principal of Change. February 8, 2018, georgecouros.ca/blog/archives/8056.
3. "Video Game Experts Explain What Makes Fortnite So Popular—and Profitable," NBC News, July 25, 2018. nbcnews.com/video/fortnite-fenomenon-what-makes-a-free-to-play-game-so-insanely-popular-and-profitable-1285065795562?v=raila&.
4. "#makeitreal Archive," Participate.com. Accessed October 13, 2018. participate.com/transcripts/makeitreal/f7285330-9cee-4732-8b45-0973c3a6169c.
5. Willis, Judy M.D. "A Neurologist Makes the Case for the Video Game Model as a Learning Tool," Edutopia, April 14, 2011. Accessed October 13, 2018. edutopia.org/blog/neurologist-makes-case-video-game-model-learning-tool.
6. Catapano, Jordan. "Teaching Strategies: The Balance Between Challenge and Frustration," TeachHub.com. teachhub.com/teaching-strategies-balance-between-challenge-and-frustration.
7. Willis, Judy M.D. "A Neurologist Makes the Case for the Video Game Model as a Learning Tool," Edutopia, April 14, 2011. Accessed October 13, 2018. edutopia.org/blog/neurologist-makes-case-video-game-model-learning-tool.
8. Willis, Judy M.D., "Neuroscience Insights from Video Game & Drug Addiction," Psychology Today, October 29, 2011. Accessed October 13, 2018. psychologytoday.com/us/blog/radical-teaching/201110/neuroscience-insights-video-game-drug-addiction.

9. Willis, Judy M.D. "Rebooting the Brain: What Does Neuroscience Research Say about Motivation and the Brain?" Partnership for 21st Century Learning, January 13, 2014, P21. p21.org/news-events/p21blog/1318-judy-willis-what-does-neuroscience-research-say-about-motivation-and-the-brain.
10. Spencer, John. "What Can Video Games Teach Us About Instructional Design?"July 3, 2018. spencerauthor.com/video-games/.

Chapter 9
1. Dougherty, Dale. "The Maker Mindset." llk.media.mit.edu/courses/readings/maker-mindset.pdf.
2. Sugar, Rachel, Richard Feloni and Ashley Lutz. "29 Famous People Who Failed Before They Succeeded," Business Insider, July 9, 2015. businessinsider.com/successful-people-who-failed-at-first-2015-7.
3. Dawn, Randee. "J.K. Rowling's Original 'Harry Potter' Pitch Was Rejected 12 Times, NBC Today, October 20, 2017. today.com/popculture/j-k-rowling-s-original-harry-potter-pitch-was-rejected-t117763.
4. Sugar, Rachel, Richard Feloni and Ashley Lutz. "29 Famous People Who Failed Before They Succeeded," Business Insider, July 9, 2015. businessinsider.com/successful-people-who-failed-at-first-2015-7.
5. Sawyer, Keith. Group Genius: The Creative Power of Collaboration. Basic Books, May 16, 2017.
6. Grant, Adams and Sheryl Sandberg. Originals: How Non-Conformists Move the World. New York: Penguin Books, February 2017, 176.

Chapter 10
1. Gruber, Matthias J., Bernard D. Gelman and Charan Ranganath. "States of Curiosity Modulate Hippocampus-Dependent Learning via the Dopaminergic Circuit," Cell .com, October 2, 2014. cell.com/neuron/fulltext/S0896-6273(14)00804-6.
2. Kashdan, Todd B., Ryne A. Sherman, Jessica Yarbro, and David C. Funder. "How Are Curious People Viewed and How Do They Behave in Social Situations? From the Perspectives of Self, Friends, Parents, and Unacquainted Observers," Wiley Online Library, May 15, 2012. onlinelibrary.wiley.com/doi/abs/10.1111/j.1467-6494.2012.00796.
3. Azzam, Amy M. "Motivated to Learn: A Conversation with Daniel Pink," ASCD Educational Leadership, September 2014. ascd.org/publications/educational-leadership/sept14/vol72/num01/Motivated-to-Learn@-A-Conversation-with-Daniel-Pink.aspx.

4. citing: doubleupfoodbucks.org/about/
5. Wettrick, Don. "The StartEdUp Podcast, Episode 13." StartEdUp Innovation. startedupinnovation.com/podcast/.
6. Kirr, Joy. Shift This! San Diego: Dave Burgess Consulting, Inc., April, 2017.

Chapter 11
1. Larmer, John and John R. Mergendoller. "Gold Standard PBL: Essential Project Design Elements," Buck Institute for Education, 2015. bie.org/blog/gold_standard_pbl_essential_project_design_elements.

Chapter 12
1. Robinson, Sir Ken and Lou Aronica. The Element: How Finding Your Passion Changes Everything. New York: Penguin Books, December 29, 2009.
2. Davis, Vicki. "Passion Projects in Kindergarten and First Grade," The CoolCat Teacher Blog. coolcatteacher.com/e308/.
3. Tucker, Geri Coleman. "Max Ash: Taking Dyslexia to the Net," Understood for Learning and Attention Issues, December 11, 2014. understood.org/en/community-events/blogs/in-the-news/2014/12/11/max-ash-taking-dyslexia-to-the-net.

Chapter 13
1. Schifrin, Nick. "Pakistan's Swat Valley: 'The Land of The Terrorists'," ABC News, January 26, 2008. abcnews.go.com/International/story?id=6731636&page=1.
2. "Malala's Story," Malala's Fund. malala.org/malalas-story.
3. "Greatest Showman This Is Me with Keala Settle," video, YouTube, 4:50. 20th Century FOX, December 24, 2017. youtube.com/watch?v=XLFEvHWD_NE.
4. citing: tarammartin.com.

Chapter 14
1. khanacademy.org/partner-content/pixar.
2. Grant, Adams and Sheryl Sandberg. Originals: How Non-Conformists Move the World. New York: Penguin Books, February 2017.

Acknowledgments
1. Lahti, Emilia. The Sisu Lab. sisulab.com/sisu-about.

Image Credits

Introduction
Duckworth, Sylvia. "8 Characteristics of the Innovator's Mindset." *The Innovator's Mindset: Empower Learning, Unleash Talent, and Lead a Culture of Creativity*, xvii. sylviaduckworth.com.

Chapter 6
Juliani, A.J. and John Spencer. *Empower: What Happens When Students Own Their Learning*.

Chapter 9
CompuCom Systems, Inc. *Design Thinking*. compucom.com/services/design-thinking.

Chapter 12
Duckworth, Sylvia. "Top 10 Reasons for Students to Blog." sylviaduckworth.com.

Chapter 14
Penfold, Alexandra. *All Are Welcome*.

Bring Elisabeth Bostwick to Your School or Event

Elisabeth Bostwick is a deeply passionate and highly engaging speaker who sparks inspiration within others. Educators glean from her authentic teaching experiences and genuine approach as she connects as a classroom practitioner. Elisabeth relates with the varying needs of educators and incorporates experiences, personal stories, and practical tips and strategies educators can take back to their schools and classrooms to empower learning.

Elisabeth seeks to tailor messages to your unique event; please see her website for new updates as well. Here is a list of topics on which she frequently speaks:

* Take the L.E.A.P.; Ignite a Culture of Innovation

* Cultivating the Maker Mindset

* Fostering a Genuine Joy for Learning

* Leveraging Technology to Empower Learning

* Supporting Children as They Navigate in a Digital Age

* Empowering All Learners through Choice, Creativity, and Innovative Approaches

Empower

What Happens When Students Own Their Learning

By A.J. Juliani and John Spencer

In an ever-changing world, educators and parents must take a role in helping students prepare themselves for *anything*. That means unleashing their creative potential! In *Empower*, A.J. Juliani and John Spencer provide teachers, coaches, and administrators with a roadmap that will inspire innovation, authentic learning experiences, and practical ways to empower students to pursue their passions while in school.

Learner-Centered Innovation

Spark Curiosity, Ignite Passion, and Unleash Genius

By Katie Martin

Learning opportunities and teaching methods must evolve to match the ever-changing needs of today's learners. In *Learner-Centered Innovation*, Katie Martin offers insights into how to make the necessary shifts and create an environment where learners at every level are empowered to take risks in pursuit of learning and growth rather than perfection.

Unleash Talent

Bringing Out the Best in Yourself and the Learners You Serve

By Kara Knollmeyer

In *Unleash Talent*, educator and principal *Kara Knollmeyer* explains that by exploring the core elements of talent—passion, skills, and personality traits—you can uncover your gifts and help others do the same. Whether you are a teacher, administrator, or custodian, this insightful guide will empower you to use your unique talents to make a powerful impact on your school community.

Reclaiming Our Calling

Hold on to the Heart, Mind, and Hope of Education

By Brad Gustafson

Children are more than numbers, and we are called to teach and reach them accordingly. In this genre-busting book, award-winning educator and principal Brad Gustafson uses stories to capture the heart, mind, and hope of education.

About the Author

Elisabeth Bostwick is a multi-award-winning educator who is passionate about creating the conditions to spark curiosity and unleash creativity to empower learning. Driven to elevate education, Elisabeth speaks at both local and national conferences to support educators in their journey to foster cultures of innovation and authentic learning experiences for their students. In addition to being a classroom practitioner and instructional coach, Elisabeth has also served as a grade-level chairperson. In these roles, she works alongside colleagues to support the integration of technology to deepen learning and leverages highly effective strategies to engage and empower all learners to maximize growth. Dedicated to making a long-lasting, positive impact on education, Elisabeth participates as a continuous learner to identify how we can support systemic change and develop essential success skills to ensure learners thrive to be future ready. Elisabeth is also a coauthor of *Education Write Now, Volume II: Top Strategies for Improving Relationships and Culture.* Recognized by PBS as a Digital Innovator All-Star and lead Digital Innovator for New York, Elisabeth regularly engages with other educators to bring professional learning experiences and contributes to individual and collaborative blogs in the PBS Teachers Lounge. She's also been named the NextGen Young Professional Leader in Education and had the honor of being the recipient of the governor's Empire State Excellence in Teaching award. Above all, Elisabeth strives to serve as a model for her children. She hopes to inspire them to be dedicated to developing their strengths and interests—leading them to their passions and fulfillment in life.

Connect with Elisabeth

🌐 Elisabethbostwick.com

✉ elisabostwick@gmail.com

🐦 📷 @elisabostwick

Visit elisabethbostwick.com for updates and resources. Connect with the community of readers and learners using the hashtag #LEAPeffect on Twitter and other social media!